**St. Louis Community
College**

Forest Park
Florissant Valley
Meramec

Instructional Resources
St. Louis, Missouri

THE CLINICIAN'S GUIDE
TO 12-STEP PROGRAMS

THE CLINICIAN'S GUIDE TO 12-STEP PROGRAMS

HOW, WHEN, AND WHY TO REFER A CLIENT

Jan Parker
and
Diana L. Guest

AUBURN HOUSE
Westport, Connecticut • London

Library of Congress Cataloging-in-Publication Data

Parker, Jan, 1949–
    The clinician's guide to 12-step programs : how, when, and why to
    refer a client / by Jan Parker and Diana L. Guest.
        p.   cm.
    Includes bibliographical references and index.
    ISBN 0–86569–278–5 (alk. paper)
        1. Compulsive behavior—Treatment.   2. Twelve-step programs.
    I. Guest, Diana L.   II. Title.   III. Title: Clinician's guide to
    twelve-step programs.
    RC533.P273   1999
    362.29′186—dc21   99–10064

British Library Cataloguing in Publication Data is available.

Library of Congress Catalog Card Number: 99–10064
ISBN: 0–86569–278–5

First published in 1999

Auburn House, 88 Post Road West, Westport, CT 06881
An imprint of Greenwood Publishing Group, Inc.
www.greenwood.com

Printed in the United States of America

The paper used in this book complies with the
Permanent Paper Standard issued by the National
Information Standards Organization (Z39.48–1984).

10 9 8 7 6 5 4 3 2 1

Contents

Introduction

This book developed out of the authors' years of experience with addictions both professionally and personally. Through working with clients with a multitude of addictions, supervising interns in clinical practice, and teaching psychology classes, we became increasingly aware of the lack of a single source which summarized information regarding the different types of addictions and 12-step programs. In addition, none of the sources we found were written to assist the clinician in integrating 12-step program involvement into the psychotherapeutic process. There was no concise overview of the many 12-step programs' philosophies and individual characteristics. Our goal in writing this book is to provide the clinician with a comprehensive, practical handbook regarding 12-step programs.

This book rests on the fundamental bias that 12-step programs are helpful for most clients who are struggling with addictive behavior. We also recognize that 12-step programs are not for everyone and discuss examples of clients for whom 12-step programs may be problematic.

The scope of the book is to provide an overview of the most common 12-step programs and guidelines for the clinician.

We assume the readers of the book are clinicians or students who are familiar with the therapeutic process. Therefore, we do not go into great detail regarding application of the clinical information provided.

We wish to express our gratitude to the many people associated with the development of this book. These individuals served as mentors, critics, or provided support and encouragement throughout this process. Without them this book would not have been written. We wish to thank Bob Coffman, Russ Federman, Pat Miya, Bill White, Sandy Adler, Herb Budnick, Diana Sjostrum, Carol Francis, Virginia Hilton, and Mac Eaton for their guidance. Michael Brennan, Dorothea Parker, Dian Greenwood, Pat Miya, and Becky Crusoe provided invaluable feedback and support. The book would not have evolved so smoothly without their critical eyes and loving attention to detail. We also wish to acknowledge Jim Lair, Nancy Chenay, Teri Fredericks, Ellie Freedman, Tracey Catalde, Pat Miya, Peter McKimmin, Michael Brennan, Jeannine White, and Dian Greenwood for their love and support. They helped us believe we could write this book. Additional thanks to Jeannie Patterson, Pam Furby, and Bob Heyenca for reading the manuscript and encouraging us to continue.

We also want to express our gratitude to those who allowed us into their world, to share their pain and struggle in the effort to overcome addiction. We sincerely hope this book contributes in some small measure to help those with addictions onto the path of recovery and a healthy life.

An Overview of the Structure of 12-Step Programs

An important phenomenon of the late twentieth century is the explosion in self-help groups. The most significant growth is in the different types of, and membership in, 12-step programs in all industrialized nations. This incredible expansion is clearly in response to a societal need. In the United States, as well as other nations, the advent of technology and the information age radically changes the individual's experience of connection and belonging. There is a dichotomy; people connect and communicate within seconds with a person around the world, while increasingly feeling alienated from neighbors. As the world becomes smaller, and people more mobile, the likelihood that an individual will live near family or childhood friends decreases. One of the greatest challenges facing individuals in our society is finding a way to form meaningful relationships without the benefit of extended family and community support. This lack of continuity often results in a feeling of alienation. For many people, coping with this sense of alienation results in the development of some form of addiction. Finding a person in the United States who does not have a friend, family member, or personal experience with some form of addiction is very difficult. Professionals in the field of psychology cannot avoid working with people who have been affected by addiction. Consequently, clinicians must be familiar with the largest, well-known, and accepted self-help group dealing with addictions: 12-step programs.

The type of alienation existing in Western society today results in the need for hope, inspiration, and being touched emotionally by another human being. Clients find these elements in 12-step programs, which is one major reason for the growth of these programs in the last twenty years. Although the initial reason for attending a 12-step meeting is often to obtain information on how to stop the addictive behavior, the draw to return is usually the inspirational component of 12-step programs. It is important for the clinician to conceptualize the addict as a person who is experiencing alienation, confusion, and pain, and who is looking for solace, hope, and a new direction for his/her entire life, not just to change the addictive behavior.

The original 12-step program, Alcoholics Anonymous (AA), was developed by Bill Wilson and Dr. Robert Smith in 1935. Both men were members of the Oxford Group, an organization which emphasized the development and application of spiritual values in daily living. An alcoholic, Bill Wilson attained sobriety as a member, and began working with other alcoholics. Dr. Robert Smith, a fellow member of the Oxford Group, joined Bill Wilson in this endeavor. Thus the concept of combining a spiritual program with fellow addicts helping each other was born in the form of Alcoholics Anonymous. All subsequent 12-step programs, developed out of the AA model, are similarly structured. Al-Anon began in 1951, and Narcotics Anonymous (NA) in 1953. Additional programs, such as Adult Children Anonymous (ACA), Overeaters Anonymous (OA), and Gamblers Anonymous (GA), were founded during the last twenty years. While the programs developed in the 1980s and 1990s have subtle differences, the core principles remain the same.

The essential beliefs of all 12-step programs include:

1. Addiction is a disease.
2. Individuals with an addiction require support from other recovering, addicted members.
3. Reliance on a "power greater than self" is necessary for recovery.
4. Abstinence from the addictive behavior is the foundation of recovery.
5. Recovery is a lifelong process.
6. Helping other addicted people is essential to long-term stable abstinence from addictive behavior.
7. Acceptance of the realistic limits of being human is imperative.

The 12 steps common to all of these programs set the foundation for these core beliefs and provide a basic guide to the recovery process from any addictive behavior. One of the truly remarkable things about what Bill Wilson and Robert Smith did was the development of a program to help alcoholics that can also be applied to drug addiction, eating disorders, compulsive gambling, nicotine addicts, compulsive sexual behaviors, overspending, relationship issues, and a host of other problems.

In addition to addressing specific addictions, 12-step programs teach an approach to life that integrates Eastern and Western philosophy. The Eastern influence comes from Bill Wilson's study of the work of Carl Jung before Bill achieved sobriety. Wilson incorporated many of Jung's beliefs into 12-step program philosophy. Jung's focus on the need for a spiritual approach in order to find meaning in life, the ability to progress beyond one's past, and the desire for continual growth were all integrated into AA. There is a long-standing belief held by the Western world that if one tries hard enough, one can conquer anything. But within this precept is the subtle implication that people who are unable to control situations are ineffectual. 12-step programs depart from this Western attitude and incorporate a more Eastern approach in the recognition of, surrender to, and acceptance of those aspects of life that one cannot control. They teach members to be accountable for behavior that influences events without claiming credit for the areas outside their control. An example is a job interview. A member is responsible for his/her presentation at the interview. Arriving early, being prepared, dressing appropriately, making eye contact, and speaking clearly are all behaviors within the person's control. The aspect outside of the member's control is how s/he compares to the other applicants. The person can interview well, but if another applicant has more experience, education, or a specific skill desired by the potential employer, s/he may not be chosen for the position. Acceptance of this lack of power is particularly difficult for the addict who has been attempting to control the addictive behavior and manipulate the environment. It is a paradox that giving up the attempt to control the behavior and surrendering to this loss of control are the first step to regaining the ability to stop the behavior. This involves a very complex interaction between taking responsibility for the impact of one's actions and one's ability to surrender to the lack of control over the aspects truly beyond the member's influence.

There are many ways that 12-step programs teach the concepts discussed above. For the purpose of clarity we have identified nine components and their functions present in all 12-step programs. These components are:

1. the 12 steps
2. the 12 traditions
3. meetings
4. abstinence from the addictive behavior
5. sponsorship
6. spirituality
7. fellowship
8. service
9. rituals

THE 12 STEPS

The 12 steps are the core of every program, and all 12-step programs share the same 12 steps. The only difference is in the first step where the addiction that the particular program addresses is mentioned. While the other components are also important, the basic philosophy of these programs is contained in the steps. Members learn a new philosophy and approach to life through "working" the steps, which usually entails writing a self-reflective response to each step and sharing it with another member of the program, most commonly the sponsor.

The 12 steps can be divided into three basic categories. Steps One through Three address the addicted person's lack of ability to control the behavior alone and his/her need for help to begin recovery. Each of these first three steps is viewed independently. Steps Four through Nine focus on taking responsibility for one's actions and personality characteristics, and beginning the process of change. Here the steps are paired. Steps Four, Six, and Eight are more self-reflective in nature while Five, Seven, and Nine require some form of action as a result of the self-reflection. Steps Ten through Twelve concentrate on maintaining and continuing recovery. The steps are a progressive process, with each step building on the previous steps.

The 12 steps and what they mean, as taken from the book *Alcoholics Anonymous*, written in 1939, follow.

Step One

"We admitted we were powerless over alcohol [food; gambling; sex; relationships; tobacco; or people, places, and things, etc.]—that our lives had become unmanageable."

The concept here is that the member suffering from an addiction is unable to control his/her addictive behavior alone.

If the member was able to do so s/he would not be seeking help from a support group. This is clearer when the addiction is a substance that people put into their bodies like alcohol, drugs, nicotine, or food. However, programs dealing with sexual addiction, gambling, or relationship issues often say that the addiction is to the excitement and/or the adrenaline released in the body when the member is doing or anticipating the addictive behavior.

Most members with an addiction of any kind have tried to control their behavior in many ways. Given that this step was originally written in relation to alcoholism, the concept here is acceptance of the disease model. This approach states that the alcoholic is unable to stop drinking without the support and help of others, especially while there is alcohol in the person's system. This step is aimed at helping them stop trying to control the behavior on their own, as that has not been successful.

The second part of the step states that the member's life has become unmanageable, which again is aimed at the lack of control the person is exhibiting, at least in the area of the addiction. The member's life has usually become organized around maintaining and protecting the addictive behavior, causing significant difficulties in daily living. One of the hallmarks of addiction is denial of its impact on the addicted person's life and relationships. The second part of Step One addresses this denial.

Step Two

"Came to believe that a Power greater than ourselves could restore us to sanity."

All 12-step programs have a spiritual, not religious, base, although the concepts are phrased in religious terminology. The idea that members are unable to stop the addictive behavior alone supports the belief that some power greater than self is an essential part of recovery. This does not mean that a member of any program must believe in God, although that name is used in subsequent steps. Members can use the power of being in a group of other people who are in recovery from the addiction, or any other concept that the person finds helpful as his or her "Higher Power."

It is important to remember that the 12 steps were written by Christian men. Consequently the language is reflective of this ideology. 12-step programs accept any spiritual or religious affiliation but clearly have a Judeo-Christian bias. Agnostics and atheists are also welcomed; however, they are encouraged to develop spiritual beliefs.

Step Three

"Made a decision to turn our will and our lives over to the care of God *as we understood Him.*"

This step is again aimed at the attempts the member has made to control the addictive behavior as well as other aspects of his/her environment. These can include the behavior and/or reactions of other people as well as the outcome of events. The purpose of Step Three is to help the member accept that s/he does not have control over many things in life. The program teaches that the member is responsible for taking action but cannot control the results. If the member believes the results are in the hands of a power greater than self, it is sometimes easier to accept difficulties or events that are painful. This means that the member is less likely to seek addictive behaviors in order to cope with these life events.

Step Four

"Made a searching and fearless inventory of ourselves."

Step Five

"Admitted to God, to ourselves, and to another human being the exact nature of our wrongs."

Most, if not all, members with an addiction have done many things about which they feel ashamed or guilty. The founders of AA believed that these emotions could lead to relapse, and the primary focus of all 12-step programs is to prevent a recurrence of addictive behavior. Therefore, it is important to address the guilt and shame. Steps Four and Five are designed to begin to help the member do so. The first part of the process (Step Four) is to write a history of actions and feelings associated with the addictive behavior that has caused harm to self and/or others. Whether the primary focus is on self or others will vary among the different programs. Programs begun prior to 1980 have more emphasis on damage to others than self, although that is beginning to change even in AA. The focus today is equally on harm to self and harm to others.

The second part of the process (Step Five) is to share the written history with a carefully selected person and with the individual's concept of a higher power. Most often the sponsor is the one chosen to hear Step Five, but therapists and clergy are also commonly utilized. The essential aspect is a safe, accepting relationship between the member and the person chosen to listen to Step Five. Confession to and acceptance by another person and/or spiritual being have been used for centuries as ways to relieve human beings of guilt and shame. Members are advised not to begin this process until they have a stable support system in the program, including a sponsor with whom they feel comfortable.

Step Six

"Were entirely ready to have God remove all these defects of character."

Step Seven

"Humbly asked Him to remove our shortcomings."

Once the guilt and shame have been addressed the member needs to begin the process of character change. Just stopping the addictive behavior is not sufficient for long-term recovery. Long-term recovery also includes identifying and expressing emotions, increasing the quality of life, and developing healthier coping mechanisms. The member must begin the lifelong process of changing personality traits and thought processes that may have led, or could lead again, to the addictive behavior. Steps Six and Seven are designed to begin this process. Members are advised that no one can be perfect so an essential concept is a *willingness* to change the traits. This also lets the person know that the process will be lifelong.

Step Eight

"Made a list of all the persons we had harmed and became willing to make amends to them all."

Step Nine

"Made direct amends wherever possible, except when to do so would injure them or others."

Steps Eight and Nine are also designed to address the guilt and shame associated with past behavior. An important part of the healing process is to take responsibility for actions that have damaged another person in some way. Apologizing for hurtful behavior can be the first step in repairing relationships that have been impacted by the addiction. However, this procedure often takes time and the member is counseled before talking to anyone about how the person may receive the amends. That is done so the member is prepared for a possible negative response. In addition to confession, restitution has been used for centuries as a way of helping people resolve these feelings. Here the member takes responsibility for the behavior toward the person s/he feels they wronged, and attempts to make whatever restitution is possible. The motivations for the apology and restitution are to begin to resolve the guilt and shame associated with addictive behavior, restore a sense of integrity, let go of the part of the self identified with the addiction, learn to take responsibility for one's actions, and be able to move forward.

Step Ten

"Continued to take personal inventory and when we were wrong promptly admitted it."

The concept here is that all members are human and will continue to make mistakes. The program's belief is that prompt attention to those errors supports the new sense of integrity and prevents a buildup of guilt or shame, thus helping the person stay out of the addictive behavior. An essential part of successful recovery from any addiction is to change much of the old lifestyle. This step reinforces taking responsibility for all actions in a way that the member has probably never done before. Another important concept of all 12-step programs is that no one will be able to practice these principles perfectly, but the goal is to make an honest attempt. Therefore this step is an ongoing, lifelong process.

Step Eleven

"Sought through prayer and meditation to improve our conscious contact with God *as we understood Him,* praying only for knowledge of His will for us and the power to carry that out."

This step addresses the continuation of understanding that the member still does not have control over many aspects of his/her life. This is especially true for people in the first few years of recovery. Learning to make effective decisions and acquiring new coping mechanisms usually require a considerable length of time. Therefore, internalizing the concept that asking for help and support as a part of life assists the member in maintaining the changes achieved.

Agnostic or atheist clients will have the most difficulty with the phrasing of this step. Emphasizing meditation rather than prayer is one way to translate it into an acceptable concept. One possible interpretation of this step could be the development of a more enlightened or open attitude.

Step Twelve

"Having had a spiritual awakening as the result of these steps, we tried to carry this message to alcoholics [overeaters, gamblers, sex addicts, adult children of alcoholics, etc.] and to practice these principles in all our affairs."

There are two concepts here. The first is that service to others with the same addiction can be helpful both to the other person and to the member. This is referred to in 12-step programs as "getting out of yourself." Helping others can assist the member in feeling good about him/herself. This also serves to get the focus off the member's problems and help him/her put them in perspective by seeing that others have difficulties that are often greater than his or hers. The second concept is that attempting to use the principles learned so far in all areas of the person's life keeps the person focused on this new approach to life. Having completed all of the 12 steps the member now needs to integrate this philosophy into all aspects of life, not just those related to recovery from the specific addiction.

TWELVE TRADITIONS

In addition to the 12 steps there are also 12 traditions. These outline the structure of the programs and address such issues as the need for anonymity, the relationship to outside organizations, and financial arrangements. All 12-step programs share the same 12 traditions. The only thing changed is the name of the program.

Tradition One

"Our common welfare should come first; personal recovery depends on (program name, AA, NA, OA, etc.) unity."

The needs of the individual never supersede those of the group. The existence of a cohesive organization is considered essential for the survival of the program.

Tradition Two

"For our group purpose there is but one ultimate authority—a loving God as He may express Himself in our group conscience. Our leaders are but trusted servants; they do not govern."

At all levels of the program—international, national, regional, and individual meeting—no specific person can interpret or mandate the meaning or purpose of the program. Leaders are elected at all levels. Their function is to serve the organization rather than to make policy or exert authority.

Tradition Three

"The only requirement for (program name) membership is a desire to stop (addictive behavior such as alcohol, drugs, sex, etc.)."

This is one of the most primary principles of any 12-step program. Some programs have a stricter definition of what constitutes sobriety/abstinence/recovery than others. This will be discussed in detail in chapter 3.

Tradition Four

"Each group should be autonomous except in matters affecting other groups or (program name) as a whole."

Each group is able to make independent decisions, often referred to as a "group conscience," regarding matters specific to that group. For example, some groups in AA state at the beginning of the meeting that sharing is to be related to problems with alcohol, implying that struggles with other addictions such as drugs, food, and sex, should not be discussed in the meeting. However, each group has the right to decide whether or not to read this statement at the beginning of the meeting.

Tradition Five

"Each group has but one primary purpose, to carry its message to the addict who still suffers."

The primary focus of any meeting or group is to support new members obtaining sobriety/abstinence/recovery. Some meetings consist of members with a significant amount of recovery. The sharing in this type of group will often be focused on dealing with current life situations rather than the struggle with the addictive behavior. However, if a new member attends this group, the focus of the sharing will shift to what helped older members begin their recovery process.

Tradition Six

"A (program name) group ought never endorse, finance or lend the (program name) name to any related facility or outside enterprise, lest problems of money, property and prestige divert us from our primary purpose."

All 12-step meetings are held in buildings owned by other organizations such as a church, recovery home, or business.

This tradition is aimed at keeping the program autonomous by keeping it separate from any other organization.

Tradition Seven

"Every (program name) group ought to be fully self-supporting, declining outside contributions."

The purpose here is the same as Tradition Six.

Tradition Eight

"(program name) should remain forever non-professional, but our service centers may employ special workers."

12-step programs are conceived as self-help groups. The founders wanted to ensure that professionals such as medical doctors, clergy, and therapists were not allowed to change or influence the philosophy of the program.

Tradition Nine

"(program name), as such, ought never be organized; but we may create service boards or committees directly responsible to those they serve."

All 12-step programs must have some organizational structure. This tradition is designed to prevent individuals serving roles in the structure from having power over the program.

Tradition Ten

"(program name) has no opinion on outside issues; hence the (program name) name ought never be drawn into public controversy."

The sole focus of any 12-step program is helping individuals recover from the addiction. Any opinion on issues unrelated to recovery might prevent someone from becoming a member of the program if his/her opinion differed from the official stance of the program. Consequently this tradition prevents the development of this potential problem.

Tradition Eleven

"Our public relations policy is based on attraction rather than promotion; we need always maintain personal anonymity at the level of press, radio, television, and films."

At the time AA, the original 12-step program, was developed, the Disease Model had not been accepted by the general public. Consequently there was much judgment and shame attached to having an addiction. It was believed that identifying oneself publicly as a member of AA could compromise other members' anonymity by association. Another concern was that someone speaking publicly might misrepresent the program philosophy due to individual interpretation.

Tradition Twelve

"Anonymity is the spiritual foundation of all our Traditions, ever reminding us to place principles before personalities."

Tradition Twelve is designed to protect each individual's confidentiality and beliefs. In addition it emphasizes the focus on the purpose of the program rather than on individual differences. When a member reacts to another member's personality style negatively, this tradition encourages him/her to concentrate on his/her own recovery process, rather than his/her reaction to the other person.

MEETINGS

The awareness of the existence of 12-step programs may come through a variety of ways. Those curious about 12-step programs first go to a meeting in order to learn about the program and to meet other people dealing with the same addiction. New members are welcomed and given assistance in this process. Those who are new to the meeting are welcomed individually and asked to identify themselves at a group level. Furthermore, they are asked if they are new to the program or just to this meeting. If they are new to the program, members make a special effort to talk to them before or after the meeting, usually offering assistance in how to become involved in the program.

Meetings serve several functions. The most common initial experience for a new member is observing and possibly interacting with other people who are in recovery. This form of role modeling can be very powerful and instill a sense of hope. As the new member attends more meetings and gets to know others in the program s/he begins to experience a sense of belonging to a supportive environment. Social contact with other members grows out of the meetings. Members give the new person their telephone numbers as part of the developing support system. After most meetings, especially those occurring at night, a group frequently goes out for coffee and more personal sharing. New members are usually invited to attend a specific meeting. This may be the person's first experience interacting with others without practicing the addictive behavior.

There are three basic types of meetings: sharing or discussion meetings, speaker meetings, and step-study or other program literature study meetings. The type of meeting first recommended for the client by the clinician will be based on the assessment of the client's ability to bond and interact. Those clients who are wary of individual contact will usually be more comfortable beginning with speaker meetings. Clients with a need for connection will respond more favorably to sharing/discussion meetings. It is rare for a clinician to recommend a step-study meeting initially.

Sharing or discussion meetings are centered around a topic chosen by the leader. In addition, members can talk about whatever else is important to them. Leadership of the meeting is rotated so that a different person each week chooses the topic and calls on people wanting to share. Members are not allowed to respond directly to what another person has shared. This prevents judgmental comments or advice giving. The program term for this occurrence is "cross-talk." Most sharing meetings are one or one and a half hours in length. There is usually a core group of people that attend the meeting regularly so even in the same program different meetings often have different "personalities." This is important for clinicians to know when referring members to any 12-step program. It is usually recommended that the client attend six to ten different meetings to experience the program philosophy rather than just the personality of a specific meeting.

Speaker meetings are usually larger than sharing meetings and have one or more invited speakers who share their journey into and back out of the addiction that the program addresses. The idea is to give hope to members who are struggling by sharing the speaker's journey. Speakers are chosen from among those members who have several years of recovery in that particular program. There is no opportunity for others to share at the group level in these meetings, which are often viewed as social events. Friends or couples may have dinner and then go to the speaker meeting, or sit together and talk after the meeting.

Step studies are meetings that focus on discussing the 12 steps. Some meetings discuss one step a week and then repeat the cycle. Members may begin to attend these meetings at any time. Another form of meetings, called "committed step studies," are an opportunity for members to discuss a step, write about it between meetings, and then share their writing or awareness with the group. Committed step studies are open to all for the first two or three weeks and then are closed to new members until all 12 steps have been "worked." It may take four to six months, sometimes more, to complete this process. A benefit of this type of meeting is the degree of trust and closeness that is formed in these groups, which is similar to group therapy. Most 12-step programs also have "Big Book" study meetings. This book describes how the program works and gives examples of success stories. In these study meetings, sections of the "Big Book" are read aloud and discussed. The original "Big Book" was written for Alcoholics Anonymous and has been adapted for other programs.

Meetings are also categorized according to gender, sexual orientation, or language. In addition, they are designated as open or closed, and smoking or nonsmoking. Open meetings welcome anyone, including those who do not have the specific addiction addressed by the 12-step program. Closed meetings are restricted to members only. However, the only requirement for membership is a desire to explore the possibility that the person may have the addiction. The availability of these specific meetings may vary from program to program and region to region.

At the beginning of the recovery process it is advisable for members to attend more than one meeting per week. How many meetings depends on the type and severity of addiction, and will be discussed in detail in chapters 5 and 6. It is also common for members to choose a sharing/discussion meeting as a "home group" which the member attends every week, and where the other members come to know him/her well. This group forms the core of the member's support system and is an essential part of the initial recovery process.

ABSTINENCE FROM THE ADDICTIVE BEHAVIOR

The essential, and only, requirement for membership in any 12-step program is the desire to abstain from the addictive behavior targeted by each program. The definition of abstinence varies from program to program. In alcoholism, drug addiction, gambling, and nicotine addiction, sobriety/abstinence constitutes eliminating these substances or behaviors completely, with the exception of medically necessary drugs. However, with addictive behaviors involving food, sex, or relationships, the definition of abstinence varies greatly and is discussed in detail in chapter 3 in the sections on specific 12-step programs.

SPONSORSHIP

Sponsorship is a one-to-one relationship between a member with more experience and growth in the program and a newer, less experienced member. The bond between sponsor and member can be similar in significance to a therapeutic relationship. The member, especially in early recovery, relies on the sponsor for guidance, affirmation of progress, encouragement, support, and education about the program. It is in this relationship that most of the individual work is done. As the member establishes sobriety/abstinence/recovery a major component becomes "working" the 12 steps. The sponsor guides the sponsoree through this process. The sponsor/member relationship requires a high level of trust, a willingness to be honest, and an ability to give and receive feedback and encouragement in order to be effective. The sponsor is available, often twenty-four hours a day, for the member to call particularly if s/he is tempted to practice whatever addiction s/he may have.

Program-related decisions are also discussed with the sponsor. These decisions include how many meetings to attend, when to begin working on the Steps, and what types of service the member is encouraged to begin, as described in Step 12. In addition, members are encouraged to discuss all other decisions with their sponsor, especially when they are new in recovery. The rationale for these discussions is for the member to get a reality check on his/her often distorted and addictive thinking process.

It is important for the clinician to support the client in obtaining a sponsor. Most often the sponsor is of the same sex as the member, in order to prevent sexual issues from complicating the relationship. There are a few exceptions to this, most especially when the member has a homosexual orientation. Specific information on how to assist the client to choose an appropriate sponsor is included in chapter 5.

SPIRITUALITY

All 12-step programs have a spiritual component. The concept is that members have not been able to control their addictive behavior on their own and so what the program calls a "power greater than self" is necessary for recovery. Most clients with an addiction have a distorted view of their power over life's events. Acceptance of the inability to control these events, while taking responsibility for one's actions, is essential for successful long-term change. Spirituality, as used in 12-step programs, teaches these concepts.

Every member decides what his/her "Higher Power" is. Many people use "God" but others use the power of the group or other concepts. This is probably the most central tenet of the entire program. Seven of the 12 steps contain some reference to a "Higher Power." At the time the original 12 steps were written the cultural context in the United States included prayer in schools, and public references to "God" by political and social leaders. Both of the major religions in the United States, Christianity and Judaism, supported the language and concepts used in the program.

Spirituality can often be the largest stumbling block for people entering 12-step programs, especially those who have been wounded by a religious organization or have no spiritual belief. Atheists and agnostics do exist in 12-step programs but tend to be silent about their lack of belief in "God." In larger geographical areas an officially recognized branch of AA, "We Agnostics" follows the Steps, Big Book, and Traditions of AA without the religious overtones. Regardless of one's belief in "God" or a "Higher Power" 12-step programs have a lot to offer that is very practical. It is important for the clinician to understand the function of the spiritual component of these programs. This will be discussed in detail in chapters 2, 5, and 6.

FELLOWSHIP

Fellowship refers to the relationships that the member develops with other members. This includes people who have been in the program longer and are further along the road of recovery; others who are at the same level as the member; and as the person accumulates more time in the program, those who are newer than him/her. An essential component of the fellowship is the development of a feeling of belonging to a group that supports and nurtures the member. Often this is the first time in the member's life that s/he has experienced such a feeling. The power of this cannot be stressed enough, and is a core aspect of why 12-step programs are so successful.

Prior to entering a 12-step program most members have either become isolated or socialized only with those who supported their addiction. Attending 12-step program meetings provides a place to develop relationships with others who are abstaining from the addictive behavior. The common goal of recovery can create a strong bond. The fellowship is often an immediate source of social contact and replacement for the loss of old "friends." How to assist members in developing these relationships will be discussed in chapter 5.

SERVICE

People with an addiction are usually self-involved to a pathological degree. The concept of service to others is designed to lessen the self-absorption at first, and later assists in the development of empathy. The type of service is primarily determined by the degree of recovery. For example, making coffee for the meeting or putting the literature out are tasks usually assigned to new members. These tasks promote responsibility and the importance of keeping a commitment. Service such as facilitating meetings and becoming a sponsor are reserved for members with more progress in recovery. These types of service assist the member in his/her ability to relate effectively to others. How to integrate the concept of service into the therapeutic process will be discussed in chapter 6.

RITUALS

All 12-step programs have specific rituals to acknowledge and reinforce length of sobriety/abstinence/recovery. Periods recognized in most programs are three-, six-, and nine-month intervals, and then each year. These are celebrated by giving a "token" for each demarcation. The token given for three, six, and nine months usually consists of a key chain. The tokens symbolizing years of recovery are specially made coins. These coins are stamped with the program initials on one side and the roman numeral representing number of years of recovery on the other. Another member gives a speech acknowledging the person whose milestone is being recognized. Then that member shares his/her process experienced during the interval being celebrated. The length of time is noted on these tokens. In addition, some programs include a birthday cake at each year recognized. All of the program members sing "Happy Birthday" at the yearly anniversaries.

CONCLUSION

Participation in all 12-step programs includes: working the 12 steps adapted to the particular program; attendance at a variety of meetings; the concept of sponsorship; some form of spirituality; a sense of fellowship; an emphasis on service; and the use of rituals. Different 12-step programs have their own focus as well as specific characteristics. These will be discussed in chapter 3.

The original purpose of 12-step programs was to assist the addicted person from stopping the behavior through embracing spirituality. Over time the philosophy of these programs has evolved to include teaching people a whole new way to interact in the world. Some integral concepts of this philosophy include developing a realistic view of one's power over life's events, accepting responsibility for one's actions, making amends, living in the here-and-now, and acceptance of self and others.

Recovery from addiction is viewed as a lifelong process. The majority of 12-step programs have the perspective that there is no cure but only remission. Therefore, it follows that participation in the appropriate 12-step program is lifelong in order to stay in remission from the addiction.

2

Therapeutic Orientation and 12-Step Programs

In the late 1930s, when AA was developed, the field of psychology in the United States was in its infancy. Little was known about human needs and development beyond that conceptualized by Freud, Jung, and Adler. Therefore, it is remarkable that so much of what psychology accepts today as fundamental is incorporated into the philosophy of the original 12-step program.

If 12-step programs are analyzed from a psychological framework, it is apparent that many aspects of the program are similar to principles of most major and current psychological approaches. This is surprising as neither of the founders had any training in psychology, and most of the psychological approaches discussed had not been developed when the original program was written.

This chapter will discuss how the principles of 12-step programs relate to eight current psychological theories. 12-step programs have their own unique terminology for various concepts often quite similar to these psychological theories. The purpose of this chapter is to formulate the 12-step concepts in psychological terms. The assumption is made that clinicians are familiar with the basic components of these theories. The theories that will be covered are:

1. Client-centered
2. Psychodynamic/Object relations
3. Jungian
4. Cognitive-behavioral
5. Gestalt
6. Reality
7. Existential
8. Family systems

The authors' intention is to discuss only those aspects of the theories listed above that are in alignment with 12-step principles; we do not intend for each section to be a comprehensive overview of the theory.

CLIENT-CENTERED THERAPY

All 12-step programs embrace the central tenets of client-centered therapy: unconditional positive regard, empathy, and genuineness. 12-step programs utilize all three of these concepts. Everyone is welcome, as the only requirement for membership is a desire to stop the addictive behavior. While it is certainly true that these programs are made up of human beings, who like some members and not others, the atmosphere in the meetings is one of acceptance and inclusion. Another central part of the philosophy is that when a member shares in a meeting no one can say anything back directly to him/her. This ensures that a judgmental response is not received by the person who shared. Therefore, when someone discloses information or feelings that are shameful or difficult to say, the person usually experiences the unconditional positive regard that Rogers writes about. Because the atmosphere is one of mutual support, the lack of immediate response is usually perceived as positive rather than negative. However, other members may share their own struggles with issues similar to the one shared by another member, which then can be experienced as empathy. Members may also approach the person who shared the painful material after the meeting and tell him/her that or how they relate, understand, or are available for support. This again is usually experienced as an empathic response. In addition to these experiences in the meetings, members also talk to their sponsor or to other members outside of the meetings on a one-to-one basis. Members learn to respond with empathy and genuineness by watching the modeling of their sponsor and other members, so that by the time they are the ones assisting others in the program they have learned this skill. Therefore, the atmosphere of genuineness and empathy is passed on from member to member. Of course, this is not a perfect process. Some members have more psychopathology which may make it difficult for them to be empathic. However, the majority of people in any program have this ability so that members usually feel cared for, understood, and supported.

Client-centered therapy also emphasizes meeting the client in the moment. 12-step programs equally subscribe to this principle. This is most evident by how one is welcomed into a new meeting. When a person who is not recognized as a regular attendee comes into a meeting, s/he is usually greeted and asked if s/he is new to the program. If the answer is yes then members offer support through words of encouragement, information about the program, and telephone numbers so that the new member can call them if s/he is having difficulty with the addiction. If the person has been in the program for some time and is just new to that particular meeting then s/he is still welcomed but with less overt attention. The degree to which a member experiences attentiveness is based on the need perceived by other members and the individual's ability to integrate the response.

A belief that change occurs in the relationship is another shared concept of client-centered therapy and 12-step programs. All 12-step programs encourage members to develop relationships with a sponsor, other members, and a "Higher Power." While 12-step programs do not clearly articulate that change occurs within a relationship, all of the structures in 12-step programs incorporate this concept. For example, Step Four asks the member to identify past problematic behaviors. However, just the ability of the individual to see the problem is not enough. Step Five asks the member to share what s/he has seen about him/herself with another human being and his/her "Higher Power." Thus the concept that healing occurs within a relationship is implied and practiced.

PSYCHODYNAMIC/OBJECT RELATIONS THEORY

All of the aspects of psychodynamic theory that are incorporated into 12-step programs are related to object relations theory. The first is how the self is developed in relationship to the primary attachment object, resulting in the achievement of object constancy. One of the primary aspects of achieving object constancy is the ability to use the image of the caretaker to self-soothe. It has been the authors' clinical experience that no client with an addiction has enough capacity to self-soothe or s/he would not be addicted in the first place. People who have well developed object constancy do not need to alter their moods with addictive behavior. They also use higher-level defense mechanisms, so they are not as prone to denial or rationalization as clients with an addictive process. The way 12-step programs help members achieve a higher level of object constancy is through the concept of the "Higher Power." Members are encouraged to develop the ability to use their sense of spirituality to self-soothe. The new member is not expected to do so, therefore it is suggested that s/he go to meetings frequently in order to receive a sense of nurturing and connection which then helps the person cope with his/her feelings. This results in the development of a symbiotic bond with the program and the meetings can function as a transitional object. Once the bond is in place then the member is helped to gradually separate and individuate by moving from the position of dependency to a position of helper. This process has many steps and takes years to accomplish, as does the original development of the child. However, at the end of the process, if the person has done the work necessary, the member develops enough object constancy to use an internalized image such as a "Higher Power" to cope with feelings and curb unhealthy impulses.

Another element of object relations theory is that infants develop an internalized representation of self through mirroring and nurturing from the primary caretaker. If the caretaker is loving and mirrors the infant's experience appropriately, then the child develops healthy self-esteem, based on the accurate assessment of strengths and the ability to accept limitations. Again the authors' clinical experience is that clients with addictive behaviors have not had enough nurturing and/or mirroring. 12-step programs provide both if the person is able to bond and take in the support. There are clients who have been so wounded in childhood that they are unable to internalize the empathy and connection offered by other individuals in the program. However, for the majority of members, the negative internalized representation of self is gradually replaced with a new, largely positive one. Again, this process takes years and is greatly facilitated if the client is also in therapy with a clinician who works from an object relations developmental perspective. These clinicians generally understand the need for dependency occurring within the therapeutic relationship and 12-step program attendance as a necessary stage of development. Hopefully clinicians working within an object relations model assist the client in moving from dependency to interdependence.

One of the results of receiving enough nurturing and mirroring within the symbiotic relationship is the development of empathy. Thus if the client has enough ego structure (is not psychotic or severely personality disordered), s/he can develop close to complete object constancy from working a 12-step program in conjunction with psychotherapy.

Equally important in object relations theory is the concept of the holding environment. Psychodynamic theory states that the holding environment consists of several elements including confidentiality, anonymity, consistency regarding time and fee, privacy, and neutrality. Ways in which 12-step programs promote these concepts include:

1. Commitment to confidentiality related to sharing at meetings and anonymity create a sense of safety
2. Meetings are time-limited and held at the same place and time
3. Meetings are generally held in buildings used for multiple purposes which contributes to a sense of privacy
4. No cross-talk is allowed which is a form of neutrality and containment

JUNGIAN THERAPY

Carl Jung had a personal effect on Bill Wilson and consequently the development of 12-step program philosophy. Jung's model emphasizes that successful recovery from addiction requires a spiritual component. In developing the 12 steps, Bill Wilson used the concept of spirituality as the very foundation on which everything else rests. The concept of a "Higher Power" is cited in seven out of the 12 steps.

Jung believed that people are constantly growing and developing beyond their past, acquiring a sense of hope in the process. This concept is reflected in the structure of the 12 steps. The member is encouraged to work Steps Four and Five, admit past behavior and then move on, releasing the effect of the past and focusing on the present. The sense of hope often begins by seeing other members who have been able to recover from the effects of the addiction. As the member abstains from the addictive behavior him/herself, hope becomes more personal. While 12-step programs tend to be more concrete and Jungian therapy more symbolic in nature, the alignment in the realm of spirituality is core to both and should not be minimized.

COGNITIVE-BEHAVIORAL

The most fundamental concept shared by cognitive-behavioral psychotherapy and 12-step programs is that changing the primary belief system and behaviors is essential for growth. Steps One, Two, and Three are about adopting a new belief system and the remaining steps focus on a process to change behaviors and concretize these new beliefs.

Other central tenets of cognitive-behavioral psychotherapy used in 12-step programs are that thoughts affect feelings, feelings affect perceptions, and changing thoughts can change the way a person feels and behaves. Therefore, changing behavior effects adaptive coping responses. 12-step programs support cognitive-behavioral philosophy by encouraging members to develop clear, identifiable, and measurable goals.

An important aspect of changing thoughts is to address distorted cognitions. There are several ways in which working a 12-step program alters a person's thought patterns. A result of working the steps can be a modification in the way the client approaches life. For example, coming to understand what is within the person's true control and what is not can fundamentally change the person's thought process related to control and willpower. Another example is that becoming part of a group which provides support to its members can alter the person's thoughts and feelings about deserving or accepting support. In addition, practicing new behaviors in a supportive environment establishes new patterns so one can transfer those to a nonsupportive situation.

Accepting that the addictive behavior has a largely negative effect on his/her life is a form of changing thought patterns. Believing that it is healthier to defer immediate gratification in order to achieve long-term results is another example of changing thought patterns. One way of addressing these distorted cognitions is through peer confrontation. These are a few of the ways that 12-step programs assist members in changing thought patterns.

In addition to changing thought patterns, members are taught to connect behavior and consequences which are often distorted in addictive family systems. Steps Four through Ten facilitate linking behavior with consequences by encouraging the member to identify the impact of his/her personality characteristics and past behaviors on others.

Another important concept is the use of reinforcement in behavior change. 12-step programs use both positive and negative types of reinforcement. An example of how both are used is the concept that time in the program and/or being free from the addictive behavior is celebrated. Using AA as a model, a member's length of sobriety is celebrated by giving a token at meetings for three, six, and nine months, and then for each year. The person is seen as a role model for others who have not abstained from chemicals for as long as s/he has. An example of negative reinforcement is when a person uses a mood-altering substance, other than for a true medical problem, and loses his/her time and has to start over. This includes identifying him/herself as a "newcomer" in meetings which means that the member can't hide the relapse from the group.

Another positive reinforcer is when the member is considered ready to become a sponsor. This decision is usually discussed with the person's own sponsor, who gives an opinion about whether the member is ready to take on this role for another person. Qualifying to become a sponsor means that the member has progressed far enough along in the process of change to have something to give to a new member. This is seen as a rite of passage, although it is not formalized. Being called on to share often at meetings can be another positive reinforcer. It is again a message that the person has something of value to give to the group. There are other subtle and overt reinforcers which are too numerous to discuss.

GESTALT

An integral part of both gestalt therapy and 12-step program philosophy is the concept of living in the moment. Members are frequently reminded that they cannot change the past nor control the future. One of the most famous slogans in 12-step programs is "one day at a time." The idea is to live in the present. Members are reminded that they do not have to decide to abstain from their addiction forever, just for today, sometimes just for a minute or an hour. So the gestalt concept of "be here now" is very congruent with 12-step program philosophy.

One of the 12-step program concepts closest to gestalt therapy is that of addressing past conflicts which are affecting the person today. Gestalt therapists believe things from the past which do not directly influence present behavior are irrelevant to therapy. 12-step programs have the same approach. Steps Four through Nine are designed to help the person work through his/her feelings about past behaviors so the associated guilt and shame do not precipitate a relapse in whatever addictive behavior the person may have had. The primary focus about the past is to change the present, and thus hopefully the future.

Becoming aware of one's self and the environment is an important component of growth in gestalt therapy as well as 12-step programs. Members who have been in a 12-step program for several years are aware that when a new member comes in s/he is usually unaware of his/her feelings, and the impact of the addiction on self and the environment. A strong focus of gestalt therapy is taking responsibility for one's thoughts, feelings, and behavior.

Much of the process in the first few years is to increase the new member's awareness of his/her feelings and the effects of his/her behavior on the environment. This is done in many ways but the most common is in the relationship with the sponsor. The sponsor gives the newer member feedback and homework designed to address this issue. The sponsor may not conceptualize giving feedback and homework in gestalt terms, but the result is the same. An example of homework which may assist a member in becoming aware of his/her feelings is keeping a daily journal where the member writes about his/her day and the reaction to it. Over time the journal becomes a way in which the member identifies and expresses feelings. It can also become a tool to assist the member in identifying triggering events and feelings that might lead back to addictive behavior. The most powerful method used in 12-step programs to increase a member's awareness of the impact of his/her behavior on the environment is working Steps Eight and Nine, where amends are made. Looking directly at the person who has been harmed and apologizing for the past behavior is an experience few members forget. Occasionally, when circumstances warrant, the member may make the amends in writing, which has less impact.

The last gestalt concept discussed is the use of the group setting. Meetings, the equivalent of groups in 12-step programs, are an essential part of the program. Here members share their experiences, and hear others' stories. The program terminology for this is sharing "experience, strength, and hope." The sharing by one member can help others become more aware of themselves. While there are significant differences between a gestalt group and a 12-step meeting, primarily due to the lack of therapist facilitation, much of the gestalt concept applies here.

REALITY THERAPY

The five essential human needs as defined by reality therapy are: love and belonging; power; freedom; fun; and survival. Love and belonging are the need for involvement with people and the need to love and be loved. Power is the need for a sense of accomplishment and achievement. Freedom refers to the ability to make healthy choices. Fun means finding pleasure in life. Survival focuses on the maintenance of life and health. This theory teaches that all behaviors are an attempt to get these needs met. Everything is an active choice. Reality therapy is a problem-solving, practical approach to change. All of the above concepts are utilized to some degree in 12-step programs.

Love and belonging can be met through the fellowship and acceptance in meetings. Hopefully the member feels like s/he is part of a group that accepts, includes, and loves him/her. The need for power can be met through a sense of accomplishment when the addictive behavior is changed, as well as when milestones are achieved in the program, such as years in recovery or becoming a sponsor. Freedom, the ability to make healthy choices, is one of the most important goals of any 12-step program, and is a major focus of the work with the sponsor. Much of the addicted person's pleasure in life has diminished as the compulsive behavior progresses and the consequences of the addiction become more obvious. Therefore, changing the addictive behavior usually brings a renewed pleasure in life once the initial struggle with the addictive behavior is over. This struggle often takes months, even years, but if the member perseveres then the reward is achieved. Survival, the maintenance of life and health, is also one of the usual results of a person who is in a true recovery process. It is important to note that many people have multiple addictions and that none of these needs will be truly met unless the person is in recovery from all addictions, not just one.

All 12-step programs have a practical, problem-solving approach to life. In reality therapy, the client is encouraged to do an honest self-assessment. Other steps include the decision to change a behavior, to make a plan, and then commit to that plan. This process is similar to 12-step program philosophy. Of all of the psychological theories, reality therapy is the one most congruent with 12-step programs. Almost all of this theory is utilized in these programs.

EXISTENTIAL

The principles of existential therapy most frequently utilized in 12-step programs include: how a sense of alienation and isolation combined with a lack of meaning impacts an individual's life; how being authentic is an important part of addressing the individual's existential pain; and the belief that human beings have free will and are thus responsible for improving their lives. In addition, existential therapists stress the importance of meaningful relationships, acceptance of self, and the client's decision how s/he is going to live differently.

Most clients with an addictive process are alienated and isolated from others even if they appear to have significant relationships. Due to the secrets that usually accompany addictive behavior these clients rarely experience a true sense of connection with others. Beginning regular attendance at 12-step meetings can help to break this sense of alienation and isolation as new members develop relationships with others who attend the same meeting consistently. Out of these deepening bonds comes the experience of connection which can facilitate development of meaning in life for the client.

Most addicted clients have been inauthentic with both self and others due to the addictive process, and thus cannot interact from the authentic self. Recovery usually begins the process of reclaiming the authentic self, reducing the sense of alienation from others, and gaining the ability to have meaning in life. This is accomplished over time by working all of the 12 steps and participating in other aspects of the program. As the person progresses in recovery and develops relationships with others in the program, s/he is encouraged and taught how to be open, honest, and true to self in those relationships. This is primarily addressed by modeling and in the relationship with the sponsor as well as making amends to others in a genuine manner.

The concept of members having free will and being responsible for their actions is another focus of existential therapy. It is up to the client to decide how s/he wants to live differently. Some clinicians misunderstand the concept of the "Higher Power," interpreting it to mean an abdication of responsibility and free will. The belief in a "Higher Power" in 12-step programs addresses the distorted sense of control, yet maintains that the member is responsible for his/her choices and actions. The addicted person has often been irresponsible and unaccountable. All 12-step programs teach that both responsibility and accountability are essential parts of recovery, thereby supporting these existential concepts.

FAMILY SYSTEMS THEORY

Systems theory is grounded in the belief that if one part of the system changes then the whole system must change in response. Most 12-step programs are aimed at facilitating individual change. However, all programs recognize the need for the addicted person's support system to change as well for maintenance of long-term recovery.

Al-Anon grew out of that awareness. Al-Anon is a program for the family members of the alcoholic. As the alcoholic changed, the spouse began either to sabotage the alcoholic's recovery or to become more dysfunctional him/herself. Therefore the need for a program for family members became clear and Al-Anon was born. Today most of the major 12-step programs, such as AA, NA, OA, SA, have a program for family members. Smaller programs recommend that family members attend Al-Anon or another similar program. Inherent in this recommendation is the recognition of the need for support for the entire system.

Another important systems theory concept is that belonging to a healthy, nurturing system promotes the individual's growth. While no 12-step program is perfect, most are significantly healthier than the member's family of origin. Most members who are successful in recovery have the experience of belonging to a group where they feel accepted and nurtured. One of the ways this is supported is through the concept of no "cross-talk" in all meetings. Members are not allowed to respond directly to anything another member shares in a meeting. They are only allowed to share their personal experience related to another member's story.

Bowenian systems theory has four concepts that are utilized by most 12-step programs. The first is that in Bowenian therapy the therapist acts as a "coach" or emotionally detached consultant. In 12-step programs this role is filled by the sponsor, who encourages, directs, and confronts his/her sponsoree. Bowen also believed that difficulties in families are multigenerational and that the person needs to become aware of the part s/he plays in the system. 12-step programs, again usually in the work with the sponsor, assist the member in changing the part s/he plays in the problem. Working Steps Four through Nine can facilitate this process.

The next Bowenian concept integrated into 12-step programs is the emphasis on separating thoughts from feelings. An essential goal of Bowenian therapy is to assist the client to develop the ability to think and feel at the same time. Once this ability begins, the client can choose an action appropriate for a given situation. Bowen's idea is that thinking is central to decisions about how to express feelings. Most 12-step programs also have this approach. In the addiction the person has been acting from impulses, not from awareness. Therefore, 12-step programs believe it is important to develop the thinking function more fully. Most of these clients have had distorted thinking patterns and have been attempting to numb emotions with the addiction.

The concept of individuation is another important part of Bowenian family systems theory and is part of the structure of 12-step programs. When a member enters the program s/he is often treated like a child, being told what and how to do things that support the recovery process. This role changes over time, similar to the transitions in a family system. As a person progresses in recovery s/he becomes less dependent on all aspects of the 12-step program. This includes attending meetings less frequently, making more decisions independent of the sponsor's or peer input, and moving into a position as a mentor to others. The degree to which individuation is supported varies somewhat between programs, sponsors, and specific meetings. One of the tasks of the therapist is to ensure the client's progress in this area.

CONCLUSION

The concept of recognizing theoretical principles embedded in 12-step programs is not frequently discussed in psychological literature. Clinicians may find this information helpful when forming their opinions about the adjunctive value of 12-step programs. It may be a paradigm shift to look at the way one's theoretical orientation could align with 12-step program principles. Many therapists draw from more than one modality. Clinicians may also use this material to integrate their own orientation(s) with clients who are attending 12-step programs.

3

Choosing the Appropriate 12-Step Program for Your Client

Most of the addictive disorders have more than one 12-step program that addresses that particular problem. Choosing the appropriate program for a specific client requires an integration of the therapist's understanding of the unique aspects of both program and client. This chapter will discuss the differences and similarities between each of the programs that addresses a specific addiction or behavior. Chapter 4 will discuss how to integrate the material in this chapter with the specific client's needs and issues, in order to make the best referral. For an overview of the structure of 12-step programs in general, please refer to chapter 1.

Each section will discuss the philosophy, attitudes, population characteristics, and specific features of each program. The programs discussed are broken down into the following categories: chemical dependency, eating disorders, sexual addiction, compulsive gambling, nicotine addiction, and family/relational issues. The programs covered in this chapter will include Alcoholics Anonymous, Narcotics Anonymous, Overeaters Anonymous, Food Addicts Anonymous, Sex and Love Addicts Anonymous, Sex Addicts Anonymous, Sexaholics Anonymous, Sexual Compulsives Anonymous, Gamblers Anonymous, Smokers Anonymous, Al-Anon, Alateen, Adult Children of Alcoholics, and Co-Dependents Anonymous. There are numerous other 12-step programs. A thorough discussion of each of these is prohibitive. The majority of other addiction problems only have one 12-step program, and even that may not even exist in some geographical locations. Therefore, the programs listed above have been chosen as the most important for discussion.

CHEMICAL DEPENDENCY

The two major programs that address chemical dependency are Alcoholics Anonymous (AA) and Narcotics Anonymous (NA). There are other programs in this category, such as Pill Addicts Anonymous (PAA) and Cocaine Anonymous (CA). However, these programs are small and often not available in other than large urban areas.

Alcoholics Anonymous

Alcoholics Anonymous (AA) is the original 12-step program, and all others are adapted from this model. The primary philosophy of AA is alcoholics helping other alcoholics to stop drinking, change addictive behaviors, and develop a new philosophy of life as described in the 12 steps. (This philosophy is discussed in detail in chapter 1.) The initial and most fundamental goal is sobriety, which is defined as abstinence from all mood-altering substances. In the beginning, the definition of sobriety was abstinence from alcohol. With the advent of the extensive use of illicit drugs, and the understanding of the concept of cross-addiction, the definition of sobriety changed to include all mood-altering substances. While many AA members have other addictions, especially to drugs, most AA groups limit discussion to problems with alcohol. This has its roots in the belief in the 1950s and early

1960s that drug users were very different from alcoholics. Today all AA members understand that sobriety is abstinence from all mood-altering substances, except when medically necessary. However, members who have problems with other substances are usually referred to another 12-step program to discuss those difficulties.

When there are multiple addictions, the belief of the majority of AA members is that the chemical dependency is the most life-threatening addiction, and thus should be addressed first. Members are often advised to wait to address other addictions such as eating disorders, sexual addiction, or compulsive gambling until they have a stable chemical dependency recovery, which may take one to three years. Therefore, some sponsors object to their sponsorees decreasing attendance at AA meetings in order to attend another 12-step program. This attitude is unique to AA and NA and prevalent even when the sponsoree is stable in chemical dependency recovery. Many alcoholics and/or drug addicts do attain and maintain sobriety while practicing another addiction. For example, an alcoholic in recovery continuing to compulsively overeat will often not be encouraged to attend OA meetings in place of AA meetings. The rationale is that any reduction in attendance at AA meetings is risking the member's sobriety. In addition, nicotine and caffeine addictions are both common and usually considered acceptable in the AA/NA culture. There is a subtle shift about nicotine evident in the increasing number of nonsmoking meetings, especially in areas of the country where smoking is becoming less acceptable.

For many years the attitude in the AA culture about the value of psychotherapy as part of recovery was negative. This attitude is a result of the fact that the psychiatric/psychological community misdiagnosed and did not effectively treat alcoholism in the 1940s through the 1970s. Many alcoholics were hospitalized for manic-depression when they were in fact chemically dependent. This attitude is changing, especially in areas of the country where psychotherapy in general is more accepted. In areas where therapy is still seen as socially unacceptable, many members still hold this belief. The tension between the 12-step and psychotherapeutic communities has begun to dissolve as therapists accept 12-step programs' value, and work more effectively with addicted clients, resulting in AA members having positive experiences with psychotherapy.

Another common attitude of AA members is that people who are not chemically dependent, called "normies," cannot understand the experience of addiction. This can create problems for family members as well as psychotherapists who are not recovering alcoholics or addicts themselves. There is also a subtle implication that only other alcoholics can help with anything related to recovery, consequently the AA member's support system must be exclusively fellow alcoholic/addicts in recovery. Therefore, many AA members will only see a psychotherapist who is also in recovery.

While AA members vary greatly in age, socioeconomic background, ethnicity, religious affiliation or lack thereof, and sexual orientation, within AA there are several subgroups that have meetings specifically fitting the members' differences. Some examples of these are young people's meetings, meetings in a language other than English, gay and lesbian meetings, and bikers' meetings. There are also meetings which are not published in the directory for members of specific professions that require a higher degree of anonymity within the program, such as physicians, airline pilots, psychotherapists, or lawyers. Some churches have meetings for members of their religious denomination, but these are not officially affiliated with AA. This is also true for meetings held for other special populations like veterans or dual-diagnosis clients.

Narcotics Anonymous

Narcotics Anonymous (NA) was the first 12-step program developed to address substance abuse other than alcohol. It was founded in 1953, some twenty years after AA. NA is the program closest to AA in beliefs and attitudes. The primary philosophy is the same as AA's, with a change in focus to drugs. NA includes alcohol as a drug so its definition of sobriety is the same as AA's current one. NA does allow discussion of difficulties with alcohol, but not other addictions unrelated to chemical dependency.

Members of both NA and AA share the belief that chemical dependency is the most life-threatening addiction and must be addressed first. Members are also advised to wait to deal with other addictions, and nicotine and caffeine addictions are acceptable. Similar to AA there is an increase in the number of nonsmoking meetings.

The attitude in NA regarding the value of psychotherapy as part of recovery is fairly positive. This is partially due to the fact that so many NA members have been in some formalized treatment program where they experienced a positive therapeutic relationship. NA members share AA's attitude that "normies" cannot understand the experience of addiction, which can create the same difficulties for family members and clinicians, and narrows the support system available to the addict.

NA members also vary greatly in socioeconomic background, ethnicity, religious affiliation or lack thereof, and sexual orientation. Due to the fact that illicit drug use did not become common until the mid-1960s, the age range in NA is not as great as in AA. As the people who began using drugs in the mid-1960s mature, the age range in NA keeps increasing. Due to the lack of generational differences there are not as many subgroups in NA. The subgroups include gay and lesbian meetings, and meetings in another language.

Cocaine Anonymous and Pill Addicts Anonymous

These are relatively new programs, started within the last twenty years. Consequently, they do not tend to have as many members with the kind of long-term recovery that AA and NA do. In addition, many clients with a primary addiction to prescription drugs or to cocaine consider themselves different than other addicted persons. Encouraging clients to attend PAA or CA may foster these feelings of difference and specialness which are actually forms of denial. Any intervention which supports the attitude that "I am not an addict like other addicts" works against treatment goals. Therefore, these programs are not usually as effective as AA or NA.

Summary

There are many similarities between AA and NA, however there are also some very basic differences. Other than the focus on alcohol or drugs, the most significant is that in general members of AA tend to be more conservative in values, beliefs, appearance, and lifestyle than NA members. When you walk into most AA meetings it is apparent that the members are part of the mainstream culture. However, when entering an NA meeting, it is clear that this group is part of a more rebellious subculture. For both programs, the definition of sobriety is abstinence from all mood-altering substances, except when medically necessary, and length of sobriety is the measure of successful membership.

When making a referral to a 12-step program for a chemically dependent client the following issues need to be considered:

1. The primary drug(s) of choice
2. The availability of meetings in your geographical area
3. The match of personality and values of the client to the program meetings in your location

Sending all alcoholics to AA and all drug addicts to NA is too simplistic and may result in the client having a negative reaction to the 12-step program that could be avoided by a more in-depth assessment.

EATING DISORDERS

The primary program that addresses eating disorders is Overeaters Anonymous (OA). Another program, Food Addicts Anonymous (FAA), has begun to develop in the last few years, but is still not widespread throughout the country.

Overeaters Anonymous

Overeaters Anonymous was founded in 1960. The primary philosophy of OA is to help members stop using food as a way to change their emotional state, change addictive behaviors, and to develop a new philosophy of life as described in the 12 steps. (This philosophy is discussed in detail in chapter 1.) One of the major differences between eating disorders and chemical dependency is that the addict can stop use of all mood-altering substances, but the eating disorder client cannot stop using food. There are three categories of eating disorders according to OA: anorexia, bulimia, and compulsive overeating. Overeaters Anonymous addresses all three of these, even though its name implies the focus is on overeating rather than all eating disorders.

Abstinence is the term used by OA to describe that program's "sobriety." It is primarily a way to provide structure around food intake. The definition of abstinence has changed over the years, and still varies by geographical region. The original definition was to eat three meals a day and to abstain from certain foods. These foods were listed on what became known as the "gray sheet." These foods included sugar, white flour, caffeine, and salt. In some regions the gray sheet is still used. In Southern California a new definition of abstinence evolved and has been accepted in other geographical areas. This definition of abstinence is refraining from eating in between planned meals, with a minimum of three meals a day. The focus is on eliminating the compulsion, whether it is not eating as in anorexia, bingeing and purging as in bulimia, or overeating for the compulsive overeater. Starving and purging behaviors are always considered breaking the member's abstinence.

The philosophy of OA is that all eating disorders are the same basic problem with a continuum from restricting food intake to excessive food intake. All eating disorders use food as a way to regulate mood. Due to physiological changes in the body, overeating tends to have a sedating effect, fasting tends to have a stimulating effect, and purging also produces a biochemical reaction in the brain. Consequently, although at first glance these three categories seem incompatible, there is actually a common denominator in the ways that food is used to change affect, and thus one program can address them all, in the same way that NA can address both the heroin and the amphetamine addict.

Another important aspect of eating disorders is body image issues. The anorexic has a perceptual distortion that when s/he looks in the mirror, s/he sees him/herself as fat despite being underweight. The bulimic has an intense fear of becoming overweight, but lacks the perceptual distortion. The compulsive overeater has an internal picture of him/herself as thinner than the reality, and avoids looking at full-length mirrors. Although OA addresses all three eating disorders, there is a recognition that anorexics and purging bulimics have such a fear of becoming fat that they may not be able to sit in meetings with overeaters who are significantly overweight. In addition, they have some behaviors that are specific to underweight members, such as starving, self-induced vomiting, and laxative or diuretic abuse. Therefore, there are usually meetings that are specifically designated for anorexics and bulimics. Since these meetings are in fact OA meetings, overeaters may attend.

OA addresses more than just abstinence. Many clinicians may not be aware of the multitude of behaviors that accompany eating disorders. These include stealing money or food; hoarding food; hiding eating disorder behaviors such as purging, bingeing, or excessive exercise; medical problems such as electrolyte imbalance, esophageal rupture or hernias, tooth decay, hypertension, etc.; and relationship or occupational difficulties related to the preoccupation with eating behaviors. These behaviors may be so severe that they can result in losing a job or major relationship. As in AA, these behaviors are addressed by working the steps, talking with a sponsor, sharing in meetings, and developing a sense of spirituality.

It is not uncommon for someone with an eating disorder to also be addicted to stimulants as a method of controlling appetite. When the chemical dependency is primarily related to the eating disorder, both addictions must be treated simultaneously. When the eating disorder presents as anorexia or purging bulimia, simultaneous treatment is essential due to the life-threatening aspects of both addictions. Therefore, involvement in OA as well as NA or AA should be encouraged by the clinician. It is important to note that most AA and NA members do not understand the health risks of anorexia and/or purging bulimia, thus AA or NA sponsors may advise sponsorees to focus only on the chemical dependency. Nonpurging bulimics and compulsive overeaters should treat any chemical dependency first then address the eating disorder after achieving a stable sobriety in AA or NA. This is also true for most other addictions coexisting with an eating disorder.

The attitude in OA regarding the value of psychotherapy as part of recovery is very positive. This is due to the fact that many members of OA have been in some form of psychotherapy that has positively impacted their lives. In addition, the psychological community has been much more effective in treating eating disorders without a 12-step program than chemical dependency. OA members do not primarily seek recovering psychotherapists as do alcoholics and addicts, but do restrict the rest of their support system primarily to other members. Due to the fact that a large percentage of the population in the United States has issues with food, there is less of an attitude in OA that "normies" cannot understand eating disorders.

Overeaters Anonymous members vary greatly in age, socioeconomic background, ethnicity, religious affiliation or lack thereof, and sexual orientation. However, within OA there are far fewer specialty meetings than in AA. In large urban areas there may be meetings in other languages and meetings designated primarily for the gay and lesbian members. In less populated areas none of the above special meetings may exist, including those for anorexic and bulimic members. The only profession that needs anonymity within the program is psychotherapy. Due to the fact that OA is a smaller program than AA or NA, therapists who have an eating disorder have greater difficulty finding meetings where they will not interact with their clients. Therefore, large urban areas may have unpublished meetings for therapists.

Food Addicts Anonymous

Food Addicts Anonymous (FAA) began in geographical regions where OA was no longer using the gray sheet as one of the guidelines for abstinence. Some OA members discovered that they were truly unable to eat foods containing sugar, white flour, and caffeine without triggering a binge. Although OA does not prevent members from eliminating specific foods from their plan, some people had trouble maintaining abstinence without the external structure of the gray sheet guidelines. FAA defines abstinence as eating planned meals and eliminating sugar, white flour, and caffeine completely. One of the problems with this approach is that members are not as likely to develop an internal regulation as quickly or at all, because they are continually relying on an external structure. The way FAA differs from OA is in the definition of abstinence and the size of the program. This also means that FAA does not have meetings for subgroups within the program.

Summary

Defining abstinence is complicated and difficult with eating disorders. There is no one definition that fits every OA member as in AA and NA. Variables such as food allergies, metabolism, activity level, body type, lifestyle, and other medical conditions need to be taken into consideration for each individual when defining abstinence. OA and FAA do not address these issues to the extent necessary. For example, there are often no guidelines for members to determine the size of a meal that takes the above variables into consideration. Medical research findings and societal attitudes contribute to the confusion related to defining abstinence. In contrast to AA and NA, OA members cannot just abstain from the substance that causes problems. There is a saying in OA that AA members "can put the tiger in a cage," but that OA members "have to take the tiger for a walk three times a day." However, many clients can benefit from the support provided by OA or FAA.

For the majority of clients OA is the program of choice due to the individualized definition of abstinence allowed in that program. Clients with food allergies to sugar, white flour and/or caffeine may do better in FAA due to the support for eliminating these foods completely. Clients with an internal locus of control, who resist external rules, will not do as well in FAA as they will in OA. Conversely, clients who need/want greater external structure may progress faster in FAA than OA.

SEXUAL ADDICTION

There are several 12-step programs that address sexual addiction. The various programs developed independently, often without any knowledge of the others. The differences have much to do with the variety and complexity of this addiction. Conceptualizing compulsive sexual behavior as an addiction originated in the 1970s and was primarily male-focused. It is more difficult to identify sexual compulsivity in women. Westernized society places more restrictions on women's sexuality, resulting in covertly acting out behaviors. Consequently compulsive behaviors such as voyeurism, use of pornography, phone sex, and use of prostitutes are predominately male behaviors.

It is only recently that sexual compulsivity has been recognized as an addiction by the professional mental health community. This concept is still controversial. Some clinicians deny its existence. The rationale for conceptualizing sexual compulsivity as an addiction is the existence of a physiological component to sex and/or love addiction which is used as a primary way to alter mood and as a coping mechanism. Brain chemistry is altered when endorphins are released, creating a "high" similar to that induced by mood-altering drugs.

The number of differing philosophies among the various sexual addiction 12-step programs can be confusing. These programs include Sex and Love Addicts Anonymous (SLAA), Sex Addicts Anonymous (SAA), Sexaholics Anonymous (SA), and Sexual Compulsives Anonymous (SCA). Availability of these programs may vary from region to region. Although each of the above programs treats sexual compulsivity differently, the primary philosophy of all of these programs includes the need to define abstinence or sexual sobriety, a belief in the value of psychotherapy, and a stronger need for anonymity based on the degree of shame associated with this addiction. Similar to eating disorders, the goal is to stop the compulsive nature of the sexual behavior and to develop a healthy sexuality. Although each program varies to some degree in its definition of abstinence, all of them agree that it includes stopping compulsive behavior.

In addition, all these programs encourage, although may not require, a period of celibacy. Members with a love addiction or nonvictim sexual acting-out behaviors have a better prognosis and have been treate by therapists more successfully.

It is very common for sex and/or love addicts to have more than one addiction. The most common dual addiction is chemical dependency. Often the sexual addiction is not identified until the person has been in recovery from the chemical dependency. Many alcoholics/drug addicts are promiscuous sexually while using, but stop that behavior once they become sober. It is much more difficult to refrain from sexual acting-out behavior while under the influence of mood-altering substances. Therefore, if both are recognized initially, the chemical dependency should be addressed first. The issue of safety, the sex addict's or potential victim's, determines whether the sexual addiction is treated concurrently or delayed until achieving significant chemical dependency recovery.

Love addicts may also have an eating disorder due to the preoccupation with physical appearance as part of attracting a partner. When the eating disorder is more life-threatening, such as anorexia or purging bulimia, it is clearly the priority.

Sex and Love Addicts Anonymous

Sex and Love Addicts Anonymous (SLAA) was founded in 1976 as the first program that addressed issues related to compulsive sexual and relationship behavior as an addiction. The primary philosophy of SLAA is to help members stop compulsive behavior related to sex and love and to develop the ability to be in a healthy sexual relationship. The major factor that differentiates SLAA from the other sexual addiction programs is its focus on "love addiction" in addition to sexual addiction. Love addiction as defined by SLAA is having serial relationships, being extremely dependent on one or more love objects, and/or being preoccupied with romantic fantasies. SLAA has the largest female membership of all the sexual addiction programs due to its focus on more covert sexual acting-out behaviors. The philosophy is that sex and love addictions are the same basic problem with a continuum from extreme dependence on one person to compulsive sexual acting out, all in an effort to regulate mood. Abstinence is individually defined but includes refraining from a personal list of "bottom line" behaviors which are causing disruption in the member's life.

Information about SLAA meetings is more accessible to potential members than some of the other sexual addiction 12-step programs. SLAA members are primarily Caucasian, and vary in age, socioeconomic background, and sexual orientation.

Sex Addicts Anonymous

Sex Addicts Anonymous (SAA) was founded in 1977 by several men who felt a profound need for anonymity. This need resulted in developing a screening process where potential members are interviewed in a public place prior to receiving confidential information about meeting locations. Originally SAA was separated into gender-specific meetings. However, today the majority of meetings are mixed, although this may vary from region to region. Similar to SLAA, abstinence or "sexual sobriety" is individually determined. Each new member makes a list of compulsive sexual behaviors, and sobriety is defined as refraining from all of them. This results in a wide variety of definitions of sexual sobriety, and members are encouraged to respect these differences.

SAA members vary in age, socioeconomic background, religious affiliation, and sexual orientation. The majority of members are Caucasian males, although the number of women is increasing. SAA is very open to diversity, thereby creating a safe environment to discuss heterosexual, homosexual, and bisexual behaviors. A small minority of the membership are recovering sex offenders.

Sexaholics Anonymous

Sexaholics Anonymous (SA) began in California. There is some uncertainty about the exact date of its inception. Unlike the other sexual addiction programs SA has one definition of sexual sobriety. It does not allow individuals to define their own. In SA sobriety is defined as abstaining from any sexual activity with self or anyone other than a spouse. SA has the strongest encouragement for a period of celibacy, and even states that celibacy may be a long-term lifestyle. When making a decision to refer to SA it is essential that the clinician determine that the client's values and belief system is in alignment with this program, as there is less tolerance for diversity. Members of SA may vary in age and socioeconomic background but are virtually all heterosexual.

Sexual Compulsives Anonymous

Sexual Compulsives Anonymous (SCA) was founded in 1982 primarily to address the specific issues of sexually addicted gay men. The program is open to all sexual orientations but the majority of members are homosexual males. There are an increasing number of women and heterosexual men in the program. Sexual sobriety is individually defined by developing a "personal sexual recovery plan" and is modeled on the work of Patrick Carnes, one of the best-known writers in the sexual addiction field. SCA will more likely be found in large urban areas with a large homosexual population. The membership varies in age and socioeconomic background but again is usually Caucasian.

Summary

There are many similarities between the various 12-step programs addressing sexual compulsive behaviors; however, there are also some very basic differences. The most important difference between SAA and SA is the definition of abstinence. In referring a client to SA it is important that s/he hold the belief that sex outside of marriage is unacceptable. SLAA, SAA, and SCA share the view that abstinence is individually defined. When determining which of these three programs is appropriate for a client, factors such as sexual orientation, degree of sexual acting-out behavior, presence of love addiction, and availability of meetings in your geographical area need to be considered.

COMPULSIVE GAMBLING

Gamblers Anonymous

Gamblers Anonymous (GA) is the only 12-step program for compulsive gambling. It was founded in 1957. The primary philosophy of GA is helping gamblers stop any form of gambling, changing addictive behaviors, and developing a new philosophy of life as described in the 12 steps. (This philosophy is described in detail in chapter 1.) Sobriety is defined as abstaining from any behavior where money or bets of any kind are involved. This includes obvious activities such as betting on horse races or going to gambling casinos, but also covers activities such as playing poker for matchsticks rather than money, or discussing the "odds" on anything. The actual addiction is usually believed to be to the adrenaline that is released when these activities occur. Therefore the compulsive gambler is very susceptible to transferring the addiction to any other behavior that stimulates adrenaline. Examples of this would be driving fast, skydiving, rock climbing or any other activity where there is a sense of danger or being on the edge.

Most gambling activities occur in places that serve alcohol or where drugs are available. This often results in dual addiction. When the compulsive gambler is also chemically dependent, the initial treatment focus must be on the latter.

However, if the gambling is not addressed soon after the person achieves sobriety, there is an increased chance that s/he may relapse on alcohol or drugs.

In general, members of GA do not utilize psychotherapy to address their gambling problem, but do have a positive attitude toward its use for other life problems. While GA members share the concept that "normies" do not understand the experience of addiction, they do believe that people with other primary addictions, such as alcohol, drugs, or food, can relate to them.

GA members vary greatly in age, socioeconomic background, ethnicity, religious affiliation or lack thereof, and sexual orientation. Unlike AA, NA, and OA, GA does not usually have meetings specifically fitting the members' differences. All major urban areas have GA meetings, but people who live in rural locations may have to travel a significant distance to attend meetings.

NICOTINE ADDICTION

Smokers Anonymous

Smokers Anonymous (SA) is the primary 12-step program that addresses nicotine addiction. There are other private treatment programs which may utilize 12-step program concepts but are not classified as an actual 12-step program. People are less likely to join a 12-step program to stop smoking than any other substance-related addiction. There is such publicity regarding products and private programs to stop smoking that SA is overshadowed unless a client is already in a 12-step program.

Sobriety is defined as abstinence from all products that contain nicotine. Attitudes toward the use of nicotine patches and Nicorett gum vary greatly among members. These attitudes range from acceptance of prolonged use to disapproval of any use.

When the nicotine addict is also chemically dependent it is important to advise the member to attend only nonsmoking AA or NA meetings. These meetings are generally available in large urban areas, especially on the West Coast and in the Northeast. In the South and much of the Midwest nonsmoking meetings are less available. Unless the nicotine addict has a life-threatening bronchial or lung condition, any chemical dependency, anorexia, or purging bulimia should be treated before focusing on the nicotine.

The primary method of psychological treatments for smoking cessation are hypnotherapy and biofeedback. The attitude of most SA members toward these methods is positive. It is important to note that the above-mentioned treatment techniques are not necessarily administered by licensed psychotherapists. In addition, similar to GA, most SA members' view of the use of psychotherapy for other life problems is consistent with their community.

As with the other 12-step programs, members come from diverse demographics. Due to the small size of this program there are no specialized meetings.

PROGRAMS FOR FAMILY MEMBERS OR SIGNIFICANT OTHERS

There are several programs that provide support for people who are dealing with loved ones, including friends, who have a problem with addiction. The first program to be developed was Al-Anon, which was founded in 1951, sixteen years after the birth of AA. As alcoholics attained long-term sobriety, it became obvious that family members, especially spouses, also had dysfunctional relational patterns. These patterns often threatened the sobriety of the alcoholic, and it became clear that the family members needed a support group of their own. Thus Al-Anon was born. The focus of Al-Anon is on living in the present and dealing with the issues of living with a drinking or sober alcoholic. As the recovery movement grew, the awareness of the impact of growing up in an addictive family system emerged. Adults who had chemically dependent parents had difficulty with Al-Anon's philosophy of living with the alcoholic/addict. Therefore, a new 12-step program was needed to address these family-of-origin issues. Thus in 1986 Adult Children of Alcoholics (ACA) began. ACA began to attract many members who grew up in a dysfunctional family system that was not chemically dependent. Therefore, in some areas the title of the program was changed to Adult Children Anonymous. Co-Dependents Anonymous (CoDA) emerged in 1986 as a program that focuses on current relationship issues rather than family of origin and also has many members who are not from alcoholic family systems.

Although there are many common traits among the members of the various 12-step programs for family members, as the recovery movement matured, awareness of the problems specific to each group arose, resulting in numerous programs for family members or others affected by an addicted person. Nar-Anon, Oa-Anon, and Codependents of Sex Addicts (CoSA) are examples of other programs for family members with specific addictions.

Because there is no substance or specific behavior from which to abstain, these programs do not use the concept of sobriety. Instead the term used is recovery. All of these programs measure recovery by regular attendance at meetings. This attendance commitment is celebrated in the same manner as length of sobriety in AA.

Al-Anon, CoDA, and ACA all imply that the family member or friend of a person with a primary addiction also has a disease. There is little or no evidence of the physiological component present in the primary addictions described earlier in this chapter existing in family members or friends. Therefore, many clinicians, while recognizing the benefit of a support system, have difficulty with conceptualizing these clients as having a disease other than diagnosable emotional/psychological issues.

The majority of members in these programs were either referred by a clinician or seek therapy after beginning a program. Due to the fact that most clinicians address relational issues, there is a clear alliance between psychotherapy and these 12-step programs. Consequently, there is a positive attitude toward psychotherapy among members of all of these groups.

Al-Anon

Al-Anon is the original 12-step program for family members or friends of someone with an addiction. The primary philosophy is to change the focus from the alcoholic's behavior to one's own needs and behavior. An integral concept is developing the ability to detach from the emotional chaos resulting from living with an alcoholic. Al-Anon teaches that the member is not responsible for the alcoholic's behavior or recovery. Through the ability to detach, family members will be better able to view their dynamics in a more realistic and objective manner. Because Al-Anon was developed at a time when divorce was not socially acceptable, there is still a subtle message that the Al-Anon member can learn to live a healthy life with an active alcoholic spouse. Thus Al-Anon focuses on learning to identify one's needs, fulfill those needs in a healthy manner, identify behavior designed to control and/or manipulate the alcoholic, change the controlling/manipulative behavior, identify one's emotions, and learn to express those feelings appropriately.

Members of Al-Anon are predominately females over the age of thirty-five. The majority are spouses or partners of an active or recovering alcoholic. Parents, other family members, children, coworkers, and friends comprise the remaining population. Socioeconomic and ethnic background as well as sexual orientation vary. In larger metropolitan areas there may be meetings in a language other than English.

Alateen

Alateen is a subgroup of Al-Anon for adolescents through age nineteen. Due to the age group, all Alateen meetings are facilitated by an Al-Anon member in order to provide structure and direction. It is the only 12-step program that is facilitated. The primary philosophy of Alateen is to help adolescents live with an active or recovering alcoholic or addict. Alateen provides a sense of belonging to a peer group where experiences can be discussed and the shame of living in an alcoholic family system can be shared. As with Al-Anon the focus is on the adolescent's needs and emotions rather than taking care of the chemically dependent family member. The makeup of Alateen reflects that of Al-Anon regarding socioeconomics, ethnicity, and sexual orientation, although there are more male members in Alateen than Al-Anon.

Adult Children of Alcoholics/Adult Children Anonymous

Adult Children of Alcoholics (ACA) began in California in 1986 and its name was changed to Adult Children Anonymous in many locations in 1990. Initially the primary philosophy was to address the emotional issues that resulted from growing up in an alcoholic family system. Today it encompasses any dysfunctional family system. A membership survey done in 1990 revealed that 60 percent of the active members did not have an alcoholic in their nuclear family of origin. ACA lists a number of common attributes shared by Adult Children, including: difficulty in interpersonal relationships, having an overdeveloped sense of responsibility, focus on others' needs rather than self needs, fear of abandonment, inability to access emotions, and a tendency to develop any of the primary addictions. ACA focuses on breaking the denial of the impact of family issues, reducing social isolation, identifying and expressing emotions appropriately, and resolving the grief about the lack of healthy parenting.

ACA is the most similar to leaderless group therapy of all the 12-step programs, with more permission and acceptance of in-depth emotional expression in all types of meetings. This is especially true of the committed step-studies. The structure in ACA, similar to the other 12-step programs, is that a large group of members commits to working the 12-steps together. What is different from the majority of 12-step programs is that in ACA, after the group is formed, it sometimes breaks down into much smaller groups known as "family groups." Members of ACA are aware that dynamics similar to their family of origin may arise in these groups. When conflicts within the group develop, they are processed from that perspective. The bonding that happens in these family groups is similar to that in closed group therapy . The groups stay together for the time it takes to "work" all 12 steps, which may take up to a year.

A major philosophical difference in ACA from other 12-step programs is the belief that members can complete the work needed and stop attending meetings as a healthy part of recovery. This is based on the therapeutic concept of internalizing change which leads to self-sufficiency. The decision to stop attending meetings is strikingly similar to the process of termination in psychotherapy.

The membership profile of ACA is quite heterogeneous. The members vary greatly in age, gender, socioeconomic background, religious affiliation or lack thereof, and sexual orientation. The only homogenous component is that the majority of the members in the United States and Canada are Caucasian, and therefore there are fewer meetings for specific subgroups.

Co-Dependents Anonymous

Co-Dependents Anonymous (CoDA) was founded in 1986 as a program that focuses on dysfunctional patterns in all current relationships. These relationships may include intimate partners, parents, children, other family members, friends, or coworkers. The emphasis in CoDA is on learning how to have healthy interactions with others. The difference between CoDA and ACA is that CoDA stresses behaviors in the context of present-day relationships, while ACA focuses on how the past impacts today. Similar to ACA, CoDA uses "family groups" in committed step studies. There is often not the same degree of emotional expression as in ACA, although this may vary from meeting to meeting. There is some overlap between the two programs, however, unlike any of the other programs in this section, CoDA has never been associated with any primary addiction. It has always been a program for anyone with dysfunctional relational patterns, even those without a history of addiction in the family. CoDA has an attitude similar to ACA regarding terminating meeting attendance. Population characteristics are relatively homogenous in CoDA. There are more women than men and the majority of members are Caucasian. Age, socioeconomic background, sexual orientation, and religious affiliation vary greatly. In large urban areas there may be couples meetings and/or same sex meetings.

Summary

As discussed above there are specific differences in the focus of each of the programs for family members or significant others. When referring a client, factors such as the presence of an actively addicted person in the home, age of the client, emphasis on family-of-origin issues versus current relationships, and availability of meetings in your geographical area need to be considered. It is also important to note that a client may begin involvement in one program and may then change to another as the need arises. While Al-Anon, Alateen, Nar-Anon, Oa-Anon, and Sa-Anon are addiction-specific, ACA and CoDA are not.

CONCLUSION

Choosing an appropriate 12-step program for a client requires an integration of all of the information presented in this chapter. It is more complex than merely identifying the addiction. Factors discussed in this chapter include: (1) the addiction; (2) the philosophy of the program; (3) sexual orientation of the client; (4) match between the program's and client's values and beliefs; and (5) availability of the various programs in your geographical location. Other important factors include timing, the therapeutic alliance, therapist's attitude towar

d 12-step programs, and the education of the client. A thorough assessment of all of these factors is essential. Therefore, integrating the material presented in chapters 3, 4, and 5 will enhance both the client's and therapist's experience.

4

To Refer or Not to Refer: That Is the Question! Who, When, and Why

This chapter will discuss which clients are appropriate for referral to a 12-step program, at what point in therapy to make the referral, and why these need to be considered together. In addition, the therapist's attitude toward 12-step programs and its effect on making a referral will be discussed.

While the majority of clients dealing with issues related to an addiction will benefit from involvement in a 12-step program, there are some clients who will not. Obviously the first step is to assess for addictive patterns. Once these have been identified there are several factors which affect the clinician's decision about whether to refer a client to a 12-step program, and the timing of the referral.

The most significant factor to consider is the client's ability to form a therapeutic alliance or attachment. While all clients vary in their ability to form an alliance with the therapist, some have extreme difficulty. Theoretical orientations conceptualize the reasons for a client's difficulty in forming the therapeutic alliance differently. In psychodynamic terms this difficulty is primarily based on the lack of the ability to attach and the use of a distancing defense. The etiology of the inability to attach can be either developmental or based on trauma in adulthood. These clients may experience an inability, or at least great difficulty, benefiting from any 12-step program involvement because all 12-step programs are based on forming relationships with other members. Therefore, a client whose primary defense prevents them from experiencing the relational support may feel threatened, anxious, and/or dissociative related to attendance at meetings. The probability is that these clients, if they try to comply with the therapist's recommendation to attend a 12-step program, may increase their addictive behavior and/or leave therapy. Therefore, the first therapeutic task is to address the distancing defense before referring the client to a 12-step program.

The inclination of many therapists who are familiar with the benefits of 12-step programs is to refer any client as soon as an addiction is diagnosed. This can be a critical error. It is imperative to do a thorough assessment of the client's developmental issues and/or relational abilities prior to referring to a 12-step program. For example, in the case of a midlevel functioning borderline addict with a distancing defense, until there is a strong positive introject of the therapist, the client may be unable to form any attachment with others, thereby making it impossible to obtain any benefit from attending the program. In one specific case it took five years of therapy before the client was able to even begin attending meetings. The client reported being paralyzed with anxiety when 12-step program involvement was discussed early in the therapeutic relationship. When the therapist accepted the client's inability to become part of a 12-step program, and focused on building the therapeutic relationship, working from an ego-structure orientation, the client began to make progress. It is important to note that in this case the addiction was ego-dystonic and not life-threatening.

Addicted clients with a severe anxiety disorder such as Agoraphobia or Post-Traumatic Stress Disorder (PTSD) will have extreme difficulty in a group setting. These clients will be unable to process information or take in contact due to their high anxiety level. They are often unable to simply attend a meeting. A clinical example is a client who was a Vietnam veteran with severe PTSD with Agoraphobic features. While he was in a residential program he was able to attend 12-step meetings with fellow vets. Upon discharge from the residential program, he had great difficulty attending meetings on his own due to his anxiety about being in a large group where he did not have a relationship with many members. His therapist helped him develop strategies to address his anxiety before he was able to resume 12-step program attendance outside of the residential setting.

Clients such as the low to midlevel functioning borderline or those with a severe anxiety disorder may benefit from 12-step program involvement after bonding within the therapeutic alliance. This may mean that the therapist will be treating a client with an active addictive process. There are some clinicians who believe that no therapeutic work can be done with such a client. However, assisting the client in moving from an ego-syntonic addiction to an ego-dystonic one, forming a therapeutic alliance, and beginning to learn alternative coping skills can be achieved with an addicted client. One important aspect of working with someone with an active addiction is obtaining an agreement from the client that s/he will not practice the addictive behavior in the hours immediately preceding the appointment. This means, for example, that the chemically dependent client will not use, the bulimic client will not purge, or the sex addict will not act out during the day of the appointment. One aspect that effects the possible progress of an actively addicted client is the frequency of the addictive behavior. Clients who can abstain for significant periods of time are more able to work on developing new coping skills than those who act out early in the day. These clients may need to be referred for residential treatment. These clinical examples illustrate the importance of looking at the whole individual and not just the addiction.

Another factor to consider is the client's locus of control. Assessing whether it is internal or external is the first step. Clients with an internal locus of control may have an initial resistance as well as possible difficulty accepting the external guidance that is inherent in all 12-step programs. The structure of most 12-step programs can be perceived as fairly rigid by a client with a strong internal locus of control. Early in recovery members are expected to adhere to the format of the program, and it is difficult to find meetings or sponsors that support autonomy at this early stage. It is important for the clinician to educate these clients about obtaining benefits from 12-step program involvement without giving up the autonomy they require. Clients with an external locus of control require additional environmental support in order to begin and/or maintain recovery, and in fact welcome the external structure. Therefore they need a different type of education about becoming involved with these programs. Both approaches to educating the client will be discussed in detail in chapter 5.

For those addictions or issues where there is more than one 12-step program it is important that the clinician assess which program is appropriate for a specific client. This might include such considerations as sexual orientation, marital status, value and belief systems, and/or lifestyle. This is discussed in detail in chapter 3 within the sections on specific programs.

Once the clinician has determined that a 12-step program referral is appropriate, the next step is to determine whether the client's addiction is ego-syntonic or ego-dystonic. It is imperative that the addiction be ego-dystonic because without the denial being broken the client will not accept the suggestion of 12-step program attendance. Assessment of the degree of denial is part of this process. If the addiction is ego-syntonic, then making it ego-dystonic becomes one of, if not the primary, issues in therapy.

There are some cases where the addiction would not be the primary focus of treatment initially. An example would be a client who is compulsively masturbating five to six times a day, a level-one sex addiction, whose father died last week. Part of the assessment regarding the timing of a referral is how much the addiction interferes with the client's ability to form a therapeutic alliance, make progress in therapy, or whether the addiction is life-threatening. In these cases it is obvious that the addiction must be addressed early in therapy. However, even in these cases, it is important that the focus be on the person, not just the addiction. If, early on, the focus is solely on the addiction there is a high probability that the client will abort therapy prematurely.

Another consideration in the timing of the referral is how it will affect the therapeutic alliance at this point in therapy. Sometimes a suggestion that a client attend a 12-step program will enhance the therapeutic bond and sometimes it may hinder it. A clinician may make a referral to a 12-step program anywhere in the therapeutic process. This can be anytime from the first session to several months, or sometimes even years. For example, a client who states that the reason s/he is coming to therapy is to stop drinking could indicate an immediate referral, or not, depending on the client's response to the suggestion. The client may identify the addiction as ego-dystonic but be resistant to going to a 12-step program. Another example is the midlevel functioning borderline previously mentioned, where it took years before she was receptive to attending a program. Another reason for delay in referring a client may be that the addiction is not identified until well into therapy. When the referral is premature, the disruption in the therapeutic alliance will be different with a client who has formed a strong therapeutic bond than with those who have not bonded. This emphasizes the importance of the timing of the referral.

The following clinical vignettes are designed to demonstrate the importance of timing. The focus of this chapter is on referral to a 12-step program, not on basic counseling techniques. Therefore, for the purpose of brevity, empathetic, reflective listening responses are implied or in parentheses.

The following is an example of a client where early referral is appropriate.

Client: I am here today because I recently realized that I drink too much. I tried to stop on my own and started again after three weeks. So I think that I need help with this.

Therapist: What happened to make you realize that you drink too much?

Client: I was at an office party with my girlfriend and had several glasses of champagne. I tried to pick up a coworker's wife in front of my girlfriend and she got angry and left the party. She told me what I had done the next day and I couldn't remember doing it. I asked a friend at work if he had seen me do it and he said yes. That made me think about other times that I went out partying and couldn't remember how I got home. My girlfriend said that she thought I had a drinking problem and that she thought I needed help. So I tried to stop to show her I didn't have a problem. When I started drinking again, after I had decided I would stop, I knew I had a problem.

Therapist: That sounds like that was a very important awareness for you.

Client: Yes, but I don't like it.

Therapist: I can understand that. Most people don't like to admit they have problems they can't control on their own. Drinking more than you want is the kind of difficulty that most people can't solve alone. There are several approaches to begin addressing your problem. (Obtain more history and do more psychoeducation regarding addiction. See chapter 5.) The approach I have found to be most effective is a combination of counseling and a support group.

Client: You mean like AA or something like that?

Therapist: Yes. What do you know about AA and how do you feel about it?

Client: All I know is what I've seen in movies and on TV. I really don't know much about it. Do you think it might help me? I'm willing to try anything. I don't want to lose my girlfriend or my job.

This is an example of a client whose drinking is ego-dystonic, who is motivated to address the problem, and seems receptive to a referral to AA. In this case it would be appropriate to make the referral in the first session, provided there was enough time to educate the client about the 12-step program. This process is discussed in detail in chapter 5.

Example of a client where early referral is inappropriate:

Client: I'm here because my husband thinks I have a drinking problem because I have wine with dinner every night. I don't agree. I'm not sure whether I should be in individual counseling or marriage counseling because I think my husband is the one who has the problem. He had an alcoholic mother and I think he is overreacting to the fact that I enjoy fine wine.

Therapist: You said that you drink wine with dinner every night. How many glasses do you usually drink?

Client: I have a glass while I am cooking and then 2 with dinner, and an after-dinner drink. It just helps me unwind for the day and I really like the taste.

Therapist: Is there anything other than the quantity to which he objects?

Client: Well, he says I'm irritable and say nasty things to him, but I don't think that's because I had some wine. He just annoys me. He says I don't get like that on the weekends until after dinner. I think it's because I don't get tired until later in the day.

Therapist: So your husband thinks you would be less irritable if you didn't drink?

Client: Yes, but the alcohol actually helps me relax. He thinks I should stop drinking altogether and need to go to AA. My father went to AA when I was ten and so he was gone a lot and "got religion." I liked it better when he was still drinking because he was around, played with me, and didn't preach. So I told my husband that I would come to counseling but that I refuse to go to AA.

This is an example of a client whose addiction is ego-syntonic. Even when she recognizes that her drinking is problematic, she will resist a referral to AA initially. A clinician's impulse might be to try to educate her about AA and its philosophy prematurely. This client needs to recognize that her drinking is causing difficulties in her life, develop a therapeutic bond, and try to stop drinking on her own. If she is not successful in her attempts to abstain from alcohol, then she will be more likely to be receptive to a suggestion about AA.

Here is an example of making a referral when the addiction surfaces after a strong therapeutic alliance has been formed. In this vignette the client has been in therapy for nine months. She is a normal-weight bulimic who just revealed to you that she has been exercising four hours a day, binge-eats four to six times a week, and purged for the first time last week.

Client: I have something to tell you about which I am very ashamed. I haven't told you before because I didn't want you to tell me to stop. Sometimes I can't stop eating and I feel really bad about it. But what really scares me is that I made myself throw up last week. That's the first time I've ever done that and I know that it means that there is something wrong.

(*empathetic response from therapist*)

Therapist: How did you control your weight prior to purging last week?

Client: Well, I exercise so I don't gain weight.

Therapist: How many times a week and for how long do you exercise?

Client: Oh, I never miss a day! I go to the gym for four hours or so a day. I take an aerobics class, work out with weights for an hour, ride the bike and swim. I can't stay at the gym any longer as I have to pick up Elizabeth from nursery school. My husband watches her on the weekend while I go so sometimes I can stay later then. Lately he's been getting really annoyed about it.

Therapist: So it sounds like you spend a lot of time each day worrying about how much food you eat and gaining weight.

Client: When you put it like that, I guess so.

Therapist: So the purging you did last week wasn't really the start of the problem.

(Client and Therapist discuss history of bulimia. Client now realizes that she has had bulimia since adolescence.)

Therapist: Have you ever heard of Overeaters Anonymous? (Might refer to Food Addicts Anonymous if appropriate. Refer to chapter 3 for that information.)

Client: Do you really think I'm that bad? Isn't that for really fat people? I'm not like that.

Therapist: I know the name Overeaters Anonymous seems to imply that the program is for people with a weight problem. But in reality there are many normal weight and underweight members. There are meetings specifically for anorexics and bulimics and most of them are not overweight. As you know, someone can have a problem with food and look like they don't.

Client: Yes, I do know that. But you've been the one who has helped me so far. Can't you help me with this? I trust you and know you won't steer me wrong.

Therapist: I'm glad you've found our work together helpful. However, sometimes it's important to have additional support. I certainly will be part of helping you with your problem with food. In my experience talking with other people who are having a similar problem provides a kind of support that I can't offer.

Client: I'm scared to go somewhere I don't know anyone and talk about these problems. You're the first person I've ever told and it took me nine months to tell you. How can I go to a group of strangers and tell them about this?

Therapist: I hear how hard it was for you to tell me.

Client: That's right. This is one of the hardest things I've ever done. I am really ashamed of my lack of control over food.

Therapist: I understand. What do you feel now that you've told me? What do you imagine my response is to you telling me?

Client: I feel better. It's nice to not have this a secret from you. I know you won't judge me.

Therapist: Can you imagine what it would be like to have this experience with other people who know what it's like to be in your shoes?

Client: It would probably feel pretty good. I just can't imagine that happening. My family would never understand.

Therapist: All of the members of (OA or FAA) have had the same experience. They have all come into a group where they did not know anyone and felt alone with their problem. That's part of the power of a 12-step program. Sharing the fear and shame reduces the sense that you are alone with your problem.

Client: It still sounds scary but I am really sick of hiding this. It's so much work.

Therapist: I truly think this could be helpful for you.

(Therapist educates client about 12-step program, including potential difficulties client may experience. This may take more than one session and is discussed in detail in chapter 5.)

This vignette demonstrates how to help clients who are just recognizing their addiction within the context of an already established therapeutic alliance. Clients who have a strong positive transference will have a different kind of resistance than new clients being referred to a 12-step program. This resistance is often related to wanting the therapist to be the primary helper. It is clear that the therapist will not be able to maintain the idealized transference position indefinitely and this could negatively impact the client's recovery from the addiction.

The therapist's attitude toward 12-step programs may consciously or unconsciously affect both the timing and competence in referring the client. As previously discussed, those therapists who strongly believe in the benefits, particularly those who are in recovery themselves, may make a premature referral, resulting in the client becoming more resistant than if the referral is made later. The opposite problem is when the therapist is biased against 12-step programs. The reasons for the bias may vary greatly, but for the purpose of this book, the result is the same, the integration of 12-step programs and therapy does not occur. Obviously when the therapist does not believe that 12-step programs are helpful to clients who are also in therapy, the therapist is not going to encourage a referral. Therapists who are ambivalent about referring to 12-step programs, either because of lack of information or some previous negative experience, are most susceptible to errors in timing and/or countertransference. Timing errors may be a result of hesitation or anxiety about the referral. This may mean that the referral is made too quickly in the anxiety. Hesitation may result in the therapist overlooking the client's receptivity to a referral. A therapist who is anxious about 12-step referrals may refer too quickly or emphatically. A combination of hesitancy and anxiety can result in the referral being made in a way that subtly supports the client's resistance. The following is a vignette where the therapist is hesitant to refer to a 12-step program due to lack of information.

Client: I thought about what you said last week and talked to my wife and I think I do have a drug problem. I guess smoking pot every day after work is too much. So I'm ready to do something about it. So what do you suggest?

Therapist: Well, there are several ways to address this. We could negotiate a contract regarding your smoking pot, we can discuss how you can build a support system, and we need to address the underlying issues and build new coping skills.

Client: Whatever you think is best. I trust your judgment. You helped me see that this is a problem in the first place.

(Therapist begins to discuss the contract and using family members for support, missing the opportunity to introduce the concept of AA or NA attendance. The therapist may even intend to refer this client at a later time once the contract is in place, new coping skills have been taught, and/or family support has been established.)

The point of the vignette is to illustrate the missed opportunity to begin to integrate therapy and 12-step work due to the therapist's hesitancy rather than client resistance. The next vignette shows what might happen if the therapist made the referral despite the hesitation.

Client: I thought about what you said last week and talked to my wife and I think I do have a drug problem. I guess smoking pot every day after work is too much. So I'm ready to do something about it. So what do you suggest?

Therapist: Well, there are several ways we can address this. Along with our work together you might consider attending a support group like Narcotics Anonymous or Alcoholics Anonymous. I know this has been successful for some people. So it might be helpful for you to contact the local chapter and find out where there is a meeting near you.

Client: I thought you might suggest that. I've seen in movies and on TV that people with a problem like mine go to these meetings. I'm glad that you think that might help me. I'll call them today.

The therapist in this example is still hesitant and does not strongly suggest the 12-step program; however, the therapist is also aware of the client's receptivity to suggestions regarding treatment. This results in making the referral even when the therapist is ambivalent.

Another factor which may affect the timing of a referral is countertransference. An example of this would be a therapist who has difficulty making suggestions to a client about things that s/he does not feel competent processing. The therapist's issues about looking unknowledgeable might delay the referral. Hopefully, this book will provide enough information so that therapists who are hesitant or anxious about referring clients to 12-step programs will feel more competent making a referral.

CONCLUSION

It is important to integrate all of the factors discussed in this chapter when considering when and why to refer a specific client to any 12-step program. As this chapter illustrates, the decision to refer a client to a 12-step program can be complex and delicate. Issues such as the client's ability to form a therapeutic alliance, locus of control, other diagnoses, whether the addiction is ego-syntonic or ego-dystonic, and how the referral will impact the therapeutic bond must be considered as the clinician determines when and how to suggest a 12-step program.

5

Educating the Client

Once the clinician has decided to refer a client to a 12-step program s/he is then faced with educating the client effectively so that the experience supports the client's therapeutic progress. The information in this chapter must be integrated with the material discussed in chapter 4. The focus of the previous chapter was on evaluating the client's appropriateness for a 12-step program referral, and the timing of that referral. An in-depth discussion of breaking through the denial system and assisting the client in accepting the reality of being addicted is beyond the scope of this book. The premise for this chapter is that the client is ready for the 12-step program referral. This chapter will focus on the detailed information the clinician needs in order to proceed through the referral process smoothly. The major topics that the clinician will need to consider include:

1. Rationale for attending a 12-step program
2. General description of the program
3. Types of meetings

4. How to find a meeting

5. Attending the first few meetings

6. The concept of spirituality

7. Sponsorship

8. The fellowship

9. Working the 12-steps

10. Addressing client's individuality within the program

It is then the clinician's responsibility to integrate all of these elements while educating the client.

RATIONALE

Once the clinician has determined that the client is appropriate for referral to a 12-step program, conveying the benefits of participation in order to enlist the client in the treatment plan becomes the next step. Therefore, educating the client as to the advantages of investigating a 12-step program will hopefully motivate the client to begin this process.

While there are many benefits in attending 12-step programs, the one with which clients most identify is the need for support while stopping the addictive behavior. Also important for the client is the presence of others who are in, and can speak firsthand about, the process of recovery. Most clients with an addiction have organized their lives around the addictive behaviors and patterns. Therefore, 12-step program involvement becomes important in replacing the time spent on the addiction with something related to recovery from that addiction. The impact of each of these reasons will vary from client to client.

A way to begin educating the client is to describe how stopping any behavior requires support. By its very definition, addiction means that the client is preoccupied with, and spends a great deal of time on, behavior related to the addictive process. For the client whose primary coping mechanisms require change, the degree of support needed is much greater than can be provided by one individual. Imparting this information can elicit questions from the client such as why the therapist is not able to provide all of the support needed. This is particularly true for clients who have a strong positive transference to the therapist. It is important for the therapist to describe the real limitations of the therapeutic relationship and the magnitude of the support necessary in early recovery. Once the therapist has described the need for additional support s/he can then introduce the idea that one way of attaining such support is participation in a 12-step program.

The next step is informing the client of the variety of ways that 12-step programs provide support. One of the most significant ways is that larger programs in urban areas provide meetings throughout the day, seven days a week. Therefore, if the client has an urge to act out, s/he can go to a meeting instead. Smaller programs or certain geographical areas may not have this availability. However, part of the culture in all of the programs includes members giving other members their phone numbers to call when the person is experiencing difficulty, thereby providing support twenty-four hours a day. Part of the task of the therapist is to help the client understand that recovery is a process of several years. Educating and supporting the client in this process can be an important part of the therapist's role in assisting the client to be successful in bonding to the 12-step program.

The therapist may also educate the client about the benefits of people with similar experiences in their ability to assist others, as often happens in homogenous group therapy. In 12-step programs, the people who provide the support understand the impulse to act out from their own experience. In addition, 12-step program members who are successful in recovery have had to develop and use new coping mechanisms which they can pass along to the client. They can give concrete and specific suggestions when the client is in immediate need. This underscores the importance of having access to relationships with people who have had the same or similar addictive behavior. As most psychotherapists are not in recovery from the specific addiction with which the client is struggling, and cannot be available twenty-four hours a day, seven days a week, participation in a 12-step program allows the client to remain with the therapist and still get this kind of support.

Finally, in discussing the rationale for participation in a 12-step program, the therapist must look at the time spent by the client on behavior related to the addictive process. The therapist cannot expect the client to give up the addictive behavior without having something with which to replace it. The client can begin to shift from being organized around the addictive behavior and replace it with being organized around recovery through involvement in a 12-step program. It is important that the therapist understand and support this process. The first step is to ascertain the time of day and the amount of time the client spends in a week performing any behaviors related to the addiction. This includes rituals related to, preoccupation with, obtaining access to, and actually doing the behavior. Obtaining this information will allow the therapist to assist the client in determining the time of day and number of meetings the client should attend in the beginning. For example an alcoholic who begins drinking at lunch every day will usually benefit from attending a daily lunch meeting. An alcoholic who does not drink until after dinner, but drinks on a daily basis, will find it more helpful to attend a nightly meeting. It is important for the therapist to help the client understand that, at least in early recovery, s/he must spend close to an equal amount of time on recovery that s/he spent in addictive behavior.

The following is a vignette illustrating how the therapist may educate the client about the rationale for attending a 12-step program:

Therapist: Last time we talked about the financial, legal, and relationship difficulties that are a result of your sexual acting out. You stated that your wife has recently discovered that you have had four extramarital affairs, and have been frequenting prostitutes. You also told me that you masturbate five to eight times a day as well. How are you feeling about what you said last time?

Client: I am ashamed and feel terrible about hurting my wife. I'm afraid I'll lose my family. Please help me stop. I don't feel like I have any control over this, and I'm tired of leading a double life.

Therapist: I know admitting these behaviors is difficult. You have just taken the first step toward being able to stop acting out sexually.

Client: I'm ready to try just about anything. What do you suggest?

Therapist: In addition to our work together, one of my recommendations is that you begin to attend a 12-step program like Sex Addicts Anonymous.

Client: Why do you think it would be helpful?

Therapist: There are several 12-step programs similar to Alcoholics Anonymous for people who have problems with compulsive sexual behavior. These 12-step programs conceptualize sexual acting-out behavior as an actual addiction. You described to me last session how you tried to stop having affairs and seeing prostitutes before without much support and were not successful. A 12-step program can provide as much support as you may need. They have daily meetings where you can go and talk with other sex addicts about your desire to act out. Talking about your impulses often helps you stop the compulsive behavior.

Client: Can't I talk about this just with you? I don't think I could talk about this in front of other people, especially strangers.

Therapist: We will talk about this and it will be an important part of our work together. How often do you have an impulse to act out sexually in a given week?

Client: Usually four or five times a day. It seems like it's all I think about most days. Every time I get a new job I promise myself I won't have an affair with a coworker this time. But I end up in one almost immediately.

Therapist: So here is a good example of how much time you spend on these thoughts and behaviors. It's affecting both your work and your home life. You've also told me that you are now in debt because of paying bills for your latest mistress. So if you went to a 12-step meeting instead of spending money on your mistress or prostitutes and heard other people talking about the damage that compulsive sexual behavior has done to their lives, do you think that might help focus on the consequences of your sexual acting out rather than the "high" you get from these behaviors?

Client: That might help. I guess I do just focus on the high. I wasn't thinking about what might happen when my wife found out and that I may have to declare bankruptcy because of how much money I've been spending. I wish I could just masturbate occasionally and be satisfied with having sex only with my wife.

Therapist: Have you tried that before?

Client: Yes, but when I try to stop masturbating I feel so anxious and irritable. I'm impossible to be around unless I can relieve myself.

Therapist: So it sounds like having a place to go where you keep hearing about the negative consequences of sexual addiction might be helpful.

Client: Yes, I guess these people know what it's like.

Therapist: Yes, that is one of the major reasons these programs work. It's also helpful to listen to what has helped others to stop their compulsive behaviors. Actually much of the meeting is dedicated to sharing about what does work and the hope that people have. I think you'll find many of the people understand what you're going through because they've been through it. One of the other things this program offers is a support network. As you get to know people in the program you'll find that they offer their phone number so that you can call whenever you have the impulse to act out. So you can have support at any time of the day or night.

Client: I like that idea. I know I'm going to need it.

This is just the beginning of the education process. In this chapter, the same vignette will be used throughout to illustrate the various topics that arise in the client's early experience with 12-step programs. It is clear that this client has a sexual addiction. The next part of the process is determining which 12-step program is best suited to assist the client. In most cases, the clinician integrates the information obtained from the client and makes a referral to a specific program. In a few situations where the therapist is not able to decide between two programs s/he may suggest that the client try both to see the one with which the client most identifies. It is the authors' opinion that it is the therapist's responsibility to suggest the appropriate program whenever possible. Please refer to chapter 3 for the information needed to make that assessment.

GENERAL DESCRIPTION

The first step in educating the client about a 12-step program is to describe the program in general terms. This includes the concept of sobriety or abstinence, the overall goals of the program and the philosophical approach to living, as well as the idea of those further along in recovery helping those entering the process.

Beginning the description of a 12-step program with the concept of sobriety/recovery as it relates to the client's specific addiction is helpful. This could be a lengthy description with an alcoholic or sex addict who still has some lingering denial, or a short one with an adult child who is being referred to ACA. In the best-case scenario the client will begin to attend the program already invested in the goal of sobriety/recovery. What is important is that the therapist assist the client to accept this idea. Please refer to chapter 3 for a complete description of this concept by program.

The clinician must be cognizant of his/her countertransference issues related to the definition of sobriety/recovery. The client with whom the therapist is most likely to have countertransference is the alcoholic whose life is still intact but who is drinking addictively. This client often has a strong belief that s/he can have an occasional drink socially. There is some controversy about whether this is true. 12-step programs promote the medical model concept of physiological addiction which does not allow for social drinking after the person has reached a certain stage. When the clinician identifies with the difficulty in abstaining from alcohol altogether, s/he may have a resistance to maintaining the position of total abstinence for his/her clients. While it seems to be true that a minority of clients are able to return to very occasional drinking, this is extremely difficult to predict. Therefore, it is in the client's best interest to err on the conservative side and encourage abstinence.

The following is a short vignette demonstrating how to address this issue with a high-functioning alcoholic:

Client: I know that AA says I can never drink again, but I think once I've learned to abstain that I can have a glass of wine or champagne on special occasions like my daughter's wedding.

Therapist: Well, that may be true. However, are you willing to take that risk? You could go through all of the difficulties learning how to abstain, begin to have an occasional drink, and end up where you are now or worse. There is no way to predict what will happen. If your doctor told you to stop eating green beans and that eating them would cause you to have significant difficulties doing your job and keeping your marriage intact, would you give up green beans?

Client: Of course.

Therapist: Would you say to the doctor, but once I've given up the green beans for awhile maybe I could have some at my daughter's wedding even though you weren't sure if you would develop the problem once more if you started eating them again?

Client: No, that would be too much of a risk.

Therapist: So what is the difference between giving up green beans and alcohol?

Client: I like the effect of alcohol. I don't care if I eat green beans or not.

Therapist: That is exactly the point. It is the effect of alcohol that may lead you back to drinking addictively, and you can never be sure without the risk. So is this a risk you want to take?

Client: Not when you put it like that.

The overall goals of any 12-step program are more than just maintaining sobriety/recovery. These goals include changing the member's lifestyle, learning new coping skills, developing healthier relationships, as well as a support system. Part of educating the client about 12-step programs involves the therapist describing these goals and ways that the program will begin to help the client attain them.

12-step programs are a mixture of Eastern and Western philosophies. The Eastern influence means that most members in Western cultures find that the program's approach to living is different than their experience. The most fundamental ways are the acceptance of things outside of the person's control and the surrender to powerlessness over the addictive behavior. Western philosophy teaches that a person is weak if s/he cannot overcome or change behavior. For example, a person goes on a job interview and does not get the job. The Western view is that the sole reason the person did not get the job is that s/he did not interview effectively. The Eastern approach, after taking into account the person's performance, would propose that s/he did not get the job because it was not in his/her best interest spiritually. 12-step programs espouse this Eastern belief.

The last concept covered in the general description of the program is that members further along in the recovery process help members who are not as far along. This is not determined strictly by the amount of time in the program, but rather by the quality of the person's recovery. The clinician can be instrumental in assisting the client in discriminating between members with healthy recovery and members with just time in the program.

The following vignette illustrates how to educate the client about some basic principles of 12-step programs.

Therapist: I'm glad you have agreed to try SAA. There is some information I want you to have before you go to your first meeting. You know you will be working on stopping your compulsive sexual behavior. It is clear that having extramarital affairs, masturbating several times a day, and frequenting prostitutes are the behaviors that are causing you problems. Are there any others?

Client: That's enough, don't you think?

Therapist: Certainly if you can stop these behaviors that will be a significant change. Members of SAA may suggest other behaviors to consider but it will be your decision. For example, many members abstain from any sexual behavior for a certain period of time before beginning to experiment with healthy sexuality.

Client: Does that include sex with my wife? I don't want to do that.

Therapist: Part of what I'm saying is that it is important for you to determine what will work for you. It will be helpful to listen to people's suggestions but to know that you can make your own decisions. Some people can sound very persuasive and as though they know all of the answers. This can be confusing especially if you are getting different messages from two or more people or when a suggestion does not feel right to you. Therapy is a place where you can discuss any discrepancies and determine what is the best course of action for you.

Client: It's reassuring to know that you will help me determine what will work for me. I haven't done a very good job of that so far.

Therapist: Another part of the program is developing a different way of viewing life. You will hear people talk about being powerless over their addiction. This is not to be confused with being powerless in their lives. Does this make sense to you?

Client: Not exactly. I don't like to think of myself as powerless. I certainly believe I have some impact on what happens in my life.

TYPES OF MEETINGS

There are several types of meetings in any 12-step program. These include discussion, speaker, and step study meetings and are discussed in depth in chapter 1. Part of educating the client is explaining the function of each type of meeting and what to expect. Predicting the types of experiences the client may have decreases the resistance related to attending meetings. An example of this would be telling the client s/he may feel anxious when attending the first few meetings. Describing the variability in meeting experiences may reduce the preconceived expectation of the client and result in a more open attitude. Clients also need to know that meetings vary in size. It is impossible to predict the size of the meeting prior to attendance. Sharing/discussion meetings can vary from a few members to over forty people in the group. Speaker meetings may be as large as one hundred or more members in large metropolitan areas. Step-study meetings also vary in size from a few to many members. Committed step studies are usually smaller and more intimate. An integral part of assisting the client to have a positive initial experience is determining the meeting size which is most comfortable for him/her. Some clients will be attracted to large groups so that they do not have to interact personally at the beginning. Other clients will want the personal attention possible in a small group and will feel more at ease in that type of meeting. Therefore it is important for clinicians to inform clients about the different size and types of meetings and suggest that the client attend several meetings before deciding about involvement in the 12-step program. It is commonly suggested that a client attend a minimum of ten different meetings before determining whether the program may be helpful. The most common type of meeting first attended is the sharing/discussion meeting. The second most common is the speaker meeting. Seldom is it recommended that a client begin attendance with a step-study group. A client who does not want personal attention, and who does not want to be identified as new to the program is an excellent candidate for a speaker meeting. Helping the client choose the appropriate meeting is an essential step in personalizing his/her recovery process.

HOW TO FIND A MEETING

It is important for any clinician to know the process by which a client may find a meeting on his/her own. A clinician's knowledge of meetings will vary. Although a therapist may be well informed about a particular program, it is extremely rare to know the particulars regarding all of the meetings available in each of the 12-step programs in his/her area. The most common procedure is for the client to simply obtain the telephone number of the local chapter of the program from the telephone company, call the chapter, and ask for the location of the meeting closest to him/her. How the client actually obtains this information will vary from program to program and region to region. In the larger, more established programs such as AA, OA, NA, and Alanon there is usually a central office staffed during business hours from which the client may obtain meeting information immediately. Other programs may have an answering machine on which the client may leave a message, or receive a listing of available meetings. Another possibility is an answering machine greeting requesting a self-addressed stamped envelope from the client in order to receive a meeting list.

The programs with a staffed central office also may provide transportation to the first few meetings. The purpose of this is twofold. First, it provides support to attend the first meeting so the person does not feel alone. Second, it assists the person in finding the meeting location as well as providing the actual transportation.

An additional consideration is whether the client smokes tobacco. In most regions of the United States nonsmoking meetings are becoming more popular. This may vary from a nonsmoking meeting to nonsmoking sections in a smoking meeting.

Before the client attends his/her first meeting it is helpful for the clinician to describe the components of a healthy meeting so the client can include this criteria in finding an appropriate meeting. These criteria include a meeting in which feelings as well as behaviors are discussed, the presence of several members with more than five years of recovery, and sharing which is respectful of individual differences.

FIRST MEETINGS

In addition to finding the first meeting, it is important that the client know what to expect when s/he attends. When the client walks into a meeting, in particular if it is small, s/he may be greeted by members of the program. Once the meeting begins there will be a general invitation for anyone who is new to the program or the meeting to identify him/herself. This is voluntary but is a strong part of the culture of 12-step programs. It is important to encourage a client to identify him/herself whenever possible as this begins the process of building a support system. Members will make a special effort to talk to "newcomers" after the meeting to help them feel welcome and answer questions about the program. Clients who may be uncomfortable being approached can be advised to get to the meeting as it's beginning and leave promptly at the end. This advice is only appropriate for those clients who absolutely cannot tolerate the attention. As stated earlier, many clients are likely to feel some anxiety during attendance at the first few meetings and may need to be encouraged to make contact with one or more people each time. Giving the client permission to experiment at his/her own pace in interacting with other meeting members is an important aspect of assisting the client to build an individualized recovery program.

The following is a vignette illustrating how the therapist may educate the client about finding a meeting and what to expect. The first part of the vignette will demonstrate how to help the client choose the type of meeting with which to begin. The first client will choose a speaker's meeting and education about that type of meeting will follow. A subsequent vignette will illustrate how to educate a client regarding a sharing/discussion meeting.

Therapist: The next thing I'd like to discuss is how to find the right meeting for you. There are several things to consider.

Client: Like what?

Therapist: You have stated that you have difficulty in large groups. Meetings vary in size and format. There are three basic types of meetings: sharing/discussion, speaker, and step-study. A speaker meeting is where you go and listen to someone with significant recovery tell his/her story. A discussion meeting is where members share their thoughts and feelings about a specific topic or whatever is going on for them that day. A step-study meeting is where members discuss how to work the 12 steps. These meetings assume you have a knowledge of 12-step program principles and so I don't suggest you start here.

Client: I don't want to have to talk. I'm scared enough about going. Thinking of having to talk is too overwhelming.

Therapist: It sounds to me like you would prefer the format of a speaker meeting. However, these tend to be larger in size than the other two types. There is no way to predict the size of a particular meeting. So your choice is between a large meeting where you will not be expected to talk or a smaller group where you might feel the need to share. I want you to know no one expects you to speak the first few times. There will be a general invitation for anyone new to share but no one will pressure you to do so. Which do you want to try?

Client: I think I'll go to a speaker meeting. I'd rather take my chances on the size of the group than deal with any expectation that I have to talk. That seems even worse. So how do I find a small speaker meeting?

Therapist: SAA has a telephone number you can call to get information. Unfortunately you will not be able to find out the size of the meeting. You will get an answering machine that will give you the location of meetings. It will also give you the address of SAA where you can send for a list of all of the meeting in this area. Since you want to start with a speaker's meeting it is probably best that you send for the meeting schedule as the machine only tells the time and location of meetings, not the kind of meeting.

Client: I'll do that. I'm still nervous about going. I just don't know what to expect.

Therapist: I can understand that. This is an important step and I know you are scared. Would it will help if I tell you more about what happens at the meetings?

Client: Yes, I'd like that.

Therapist: All meetings usually start with reading a few excerpts from program literature. During that time people who are new to recovery or that meeting may be asked to identify themselves. You don't have to do this; however, this is how members know to whom they might reach out to welcome and help learn about the program. I know that you are scared about going the first time. You might want to wait to decide whether you are going to identify yourself until you see how you feel at that moment.

Client: I doubt I'll want to speak up but I'll wait and see.

Therapist: After the literature is read, members' lengths of sobriety are acknowledged. This is done for periods of three, six, and nine months, and then for each year. They actually sing "Happy Birthday" to members who are celebrating a year or more and everyone being recognized gets a token. Each member being acknowledged says a few words. After this part of the meeting the speaker gets up and tells his/her story of addiction and recovery. The speaker usually talks for about forty-five minutes. After the speaker finishes there may be a few announcements and then the meeting is adjourned. Part of the closing is everyone stands up, holds hands with the person on either side of them, and a prayer is said aloud.

Client: There's a lot that happens at these meetings. I'm glad you told me. It helps me feel more prepared. With all this activity it sounds like the focus won't be on me. So what's this about a prayer? (This will be answered in the vignette addressing spirituality.)

The following vignette demonstrates educating the client about attending a sharing/discussion meeting.

Therapist: The next thing I'd like to discuss is how to find the right meeting for you. There are several things to consider.

Client: Like what?

Therapist: You have stated that you have difficulty in large groups. Meetings vary in size and format. There are three basic types of meetings: sharing/discussion, speaker, and step-study. A speaker meeting is where you go and listen to someone with significant recovery tells his/her story. A discussion meeting is where members share their thoughts and feelings about a specific topic or whatever is going on for them that day. A step-study meeting is where members discuss how to work the 12 steps and is not a good place to begin.

Client: I don't want to have to deal with a large group. I'm scared enough about going.

Therapist: It sounds to me like you would prefer the format of a sharing/discussion. These tend to be smaller in size than the speaker meetings. There is no way to predict the size of a particular meeting. So you will probably need to go to a few sharing/discussion meetings in order to find one that is the size with which you feel comfortable. Although these are sharing/discussion meetings, I want you to know no one expects you to speak the first few times. There will be a general invitation for anyone new to share but no one will pressure you to do so.

Client: Yes. I definitely think I'll go to a sharing/discussion meeting. I'd rather take my chances on being expected to talk than be in a large group. That seems even worse. Besides going to several meetings is there any other way I might find a small sharing/discussion meeting?

Therapist: Yes. SAA has a telephone number you can call to get information. You will get an answering machine that will give you the location of meetings as well as the local address of SAA where you can send for a list of all of the meeting in this area. You can enclose a note requesting information about the size of the sharing/discussion meetings. The person who sends out the meeting lists will probably have an idea about the approximate size of each meeting and can give you that information.

Client: I'll do that. I'm still nervous about going. I just don't know what to expect.

Therapist: I can understand that. This is an important step and I know you are scared. Would it help if I tell you more about what happens at the meetings?

Client: Yes, I'd like that.

Therapist: All meetings usually start with reading a few excerpts from program literature. During that time people who are new to recovery or that meeting may be asked to identify themselves. You don't have to do this; however, this is how members know to whom they might reach out to welcome and help learn about the program. I know that you are scared about going the first time. You might want to wait to decide whether you are going to identify yourself until you see how you feel at that moment.

Client: I doubt I'll want to speak up but I'll wait and see.

Therapist: After the literature is read members' lengths of sobriety are acknowledged. This is done for periods of three, six, and nine months, and then for each year. They actually sing "Happy Birthday" to members who are celebrating a year or more and everyone being recognized gets a token. Each member being acknowledged says a few words. After this part of the meeting the leader speaks for a few minutes and identifies a topic for discussion. Members raise their hands and wait for the leader to call on them. Most members share about the topic, but if someone has an issue s/he needs to talk about other than the topic s/he may do so. Most meetings are an hour in length but a few are longer. At the end of the meeting there may be a few announcements. As the meeting closes everyone stands up, holds hands with the person on either side of them, and a prayer is said aloud.

Client: There's a lot that happens at these meetings. I'm glad you told me. It helps me feel more prepared. With all this activity it sounds like the focus won't be on me. So what is that about a prayer?

SPIRITUALITY

A client's reaction to the spiritual aspect of 12-step programs varies greatly based on his/her experience with organized religion, current beliefs, and how this is introduced by the clinician. 12-step programs incorporate the concept of spirituality which many people associate with religion. Religion is not a part of any 12-step program. In fact, 12-step program members vary from those who describe themselves as strongly affiliated with a specific faith to those who would describe themselves as agnostic or atheist, and consequently have no religious affiliation. It is imperative to explain to the client that s/he does not have to espouse any religious beliefs in order to utilize the program. The language used by 12-step programs does include the words "Higher Power" and "God." This will not be a problem for those clients with a religious affiliation. It is the agnostic, atheist or those who have been wounded by organized religion who will have the most difficulty with these terms. This is also true for the therapist, who must be cognizant of his/her countertransference issues regarding this aspect of the program.

Therapists need to be able to separate their own difficulties with spirituality as well as the terms used in 12-step programs from the best interest of the addicted client. This is one of the largest blocks to therapists referring clients to 12-step programs. Unfortunately, it is often the therapist's unresolved countertransference which is the deciding factor regarding 12-step program referral, not an informed assessment of the client's needs. The therapist's own comfort or discomfort with discussing religious and/or spiritual material in the therapeutic setting will directly influence the depth of discussion about the spiritual aspect of 12-step programs.

Clients with an addictive process, needing a referral to a 12-step program, have usually tried to control their compulsive behavior on their own and failed. The religious connotation aside, the concept of relying on a power greater than self is used to provide external support. Much of the client's lack of self-respect may be based in his/her inability to control the addictive behavior. Incorporating the idea s/he is unable to do so without the assistance of external support may help these clients break the cycle of addictive behavior. 12-step programs use the words "Higher Power" and "God" to describe part of the external support. This is the first step in a long process leading to the development of a more internal locus of control and object constancy. As discussed in chapter 2, the concept of a "Higher Power" is an integral part of developing the ability to self-soothe.

The primary discussion is usually centered around the use of the terms "Higher Power" and "God." How the client integrates and defines these terms will determine the direction of this process. The language used by the therapist when educating the client about this aspect of the program should match that of the client. Some clients may like the word "God," others may want to use "Higher Power," while still others may have trouble with either term. For example, a client with a strong aversion to religion might need the therapist's assistance understanding the concept of a power greater than self and in formulating a word or phrase that symbolizes this concept. One strategy commonly used for these individuals is conceptualizing the group of recovering members as the power greater than self. Rather than focusing on the terms, the therapist may also need to help the client process his/her feelings associated with the use of "Higher Power" and "God."

This following vignette illustrates how to discuss the spiritual aspects of the 12-step program with a client who has difficulty with the concept of "God" or a "Higher Power." It picks up at the point at which the last vignette ended.

Client: So what is this about a prayer?

Therapist: All 12-step programs have a spiritual component. You don't have to believe in any organized religion or even in a God, but part of the program is learning to rely on a power greater than self.

Client: Still sounds like religion to me. I don't believe in God and I think people who do are hypocrites.

Therapist: Sounds like you've had a negative experience with religion. Is that accurate?

Client: I sure have. My mother crammed her religion down my throat. She was always going to church and preaching at me not to have sex or swear, but she slept with my step-father for years before she married him and used the f-word all the time. She was just a hypocrite.

Therapist: I can understand how you would be angry at your mother. How does this apply to everyone who believes in a Higher Power?

Client: It seemed like all her friends were the same. My first girlfriend's mother didn't want us to have sex either, but she was living with a guy.

Therapist: So what you are describing is having very specific beliefs crammed down your throat and seeing a difference between what is said and done. You seem to have generalized this experience to all spiritual practices. The spiritual part of a 12-step programs is about needing help to abstain from your addictive behavior. Have you been able to stop having affairs or going to prostitutes for a significant length of time on your own?

Client: No, but what does that have to do with God?

Therapist: It's not really about God. The idea here is that people with an addiction need more than self-reliance to stop the behavior. So the concept of a power greater than self is used. Many people think of the group of program members who are abstaining from the addictive behavior as their Higher Power.

Client: So how does that work?

Therapist: The people who wrote the 12 steps did believe in a God so they used that word. But everyone in the program agrees that the Higher Power is anything bigger than a single person. The idea is that no one can be successful alone in recovery. Everyone needs help. The ability to admit you need and reach out for help is an essential part of stopping the addiction. Would you agree with that statement?

Client: Yes, I certainly haven't been able to stop and that's why I came to see you. I knew I needed help.

Therapist: Could you see yourself believing in some power greater than yourself even if that is the power of the group?

Client: Well, I can certainly consider that more easily than I can accept God.

Therapist: That's all you need to start.

SPONSORSHIP

Sponsorship is an integral part of 12-step programs and the key here is for the clinician to assist the client in finding the right sponsor. The primary consideration is matching the client's needs to the sponsor's style. Some sponsors are very directive and do not tolerate variance from their beliefs about what works in recovery. Others are more flexible and help the new member find his/her own way. Clients who have a strong external locus of control and/or little sense of self often prefer a sponsor who is more directive. Clients with a more internal locus of control or who have strong issues with authority figures seem to make more progress with a sponsor who is more collaborative in nature rather than directive.

It is not necessary that the sponsor and client have similar personality types as long as the sponsor understands the needs of the client. For example, the sponsor may be quite extroverted and actively involved in the social aspects of the program. The client could be quite introverted and prefer very small group interactions and thus avoid large gatherings. It is essential that the sponsor understand that this is not avoidance or isolation but is the client's personality style. The sponsor can be directive in this case as long as the direction matches the client's needs.

The client who is an atheist or agnostic requires a sponsor who is able to respect the client's spiritual belief system. The clinician can be helpful in supporting the client to interview potential sponsors in order to find one who will respect the lack of a belief in "God" as the "Higher Power." Hopefully, the sponsor will assist the client in developing another definition of "Higher Power" which fits the client's belief system.

It is equally important, especially for the client who is in therapy prior to beginning 12-step program involvement, that the sponsor respect the therapeutic alliance. Most members of 12-step programs today understand, if not encourage, participation in psychotherapy at some point in the recovery process. However, particularly in the older programs like AA, there is still much ambivalence regarding the role of therapy in recovery. Educating the client about choosing a sponsor who is supportive of ongoing psychotherapy is important. Equally important is anticipating negative comments about therapists.

An additional consideration is the use of psychotropic medication in recovery, especially in AA or NA. These include antidepressants and antipsychotics which have not been found to be addictive and are usually medically necessary. Antianxiety agents and pain medications present a more complex problem due to the addictive qualities of these drugs. Any client requiring antianxiety or pain medication needs to have his/her consumption of the drug monitored carefully. In addition, it is essential that the physician is aware of the client's history of addiction when prescribing these medications. Many members of these programs hold a rigid view that sobriety is defined as abstaining from all psychotropic substances, including any prescribed by a physician. Clients who require any of the above described medications need a sponsor who can understand the complexity of this issue and the importance for an individual assessment regarding taking these drugs.

Once the above issues have been clarified, the clinician's task is to teach the client how to find an appropriate sponsor. The first step is to help the client observe different people in the meetings s/he is attending. Discussing the ways to identify the sponsor's probable style from his/her sharing is the primary method utilized. Another way to discover information is to talk to other members about what they like or dislike about their sponsor's style. Once a person has been identified as a potential sponsor then it is important to support the client in interviewing the person. It is important to know that interviewing someone to be a sponsor is not a part of the culture of 12-step programs for members in early recovery. Role playing can be of great benefit in assisting the client with this process.

Most 12-step program members emphasize the importance of finding a sponsor quickly and may confront a client who seems to be delaying this process. One solution to this difficulty is for the client to choose a "temporary sponsor" immediately and then look for the sponsor who most aligns with his/her needs. Temporary sponsors know that the client is not making a commitment to work with him/her long term. The role of the temporary sponsor is to provide one-on-one support while the member is getting to know people in the program more personally.

The role of the therapist is to assist the client in choosing the best sponsor for him/her due to the depth and richness of this relationship and it impact on the recovery process. The following is a vignette describing the process of assisting the client in choosing and interviewing a sponsor.

Client: I went to some meetings and I keep hearing I need to get a sponsor. How do I go about getting one?

Therapist: There are several things to consider when choosing a sponsor. The most important aspect is finding someone with whom you feel safe to share your feelings and experiences. Does anyone come to mind?

Client: Yes, there are a couple of guys I think I could talk to pretty easily. One of the things I am afraid about is having someone tell me what to do.

Therapist: Is there anything in either of these guy's sharing which is a clue about whether they will tell you what to do or help you explore what is helpful for you?

Client: David seems more accepting of different ways to deal with problems. I know he's in therapy. George is nice and I like him but now that you ask about it, he can be a little dogmatic at times.

Therapist: Do you know anyone that either David or George sponsors?

Client: Yes, I know two men George sponsors and one that works with David.

Therapist: Have you talked to any of them about their experience?

Client: No, I guess that would be a good idea.

Therapist: There are a couple of other things to consider. One is their length of sobriety, their feelings about you being in therapy, and whether they have enough time to spend with you. I encourage you to ask about all of these things before you decide. It is often helpful to interview a potential sponsor.

Client: You mean I can do that?

Therapist: Yes. This is going to be an important person in your recovery process and therefore it is important to choose as carefully as possible.

FELLOWSHIP

Most, if not all, psychological theories acknowledge the human need for contact and a sense of belonging. Fellowship created in 12-step programs can facilitate movement from isolation or superficial contact into more meaningful connection. The clinician's primary responsibility is to educate the client about the role and importance of developing peer relationships in the 12-step program. How the clinician addresses this process will vary with his/her theoretical orientation.

One of the primary roles of developing relationships within the 12-step program is to help the client contain his/her impulses to act out the addictive behavior. Most, if not all, clients with an addictive process have impulses to act out many times during a day or week. As discussed in previous chapters the therapist cannot provide all the support necessary for clients to refrain from acting out. One of the most frequently used strategies to contain the impulse is to talk to another 12-step program member who is familiar with the desire to act out. Obviously a client must have relationships within the program to take advantage of this method of containment.

One of the other major reasons that 12-step programs are helpful in addressing addictive behaviors is the formation of close relationships which support the client's recovery process. A 12-step program is comprised of people who understand the need for this support. As a client begins to abstain from addictive behaviors s/he initiates a process of change that permeates his/her entire life. Many prior relationships have tolerated or supported the addictive behaviors and consequently must change in response to the client entering recovery, or the client will eventually withdraw from that relationship. In order for the client to begin to eliminate those relationships that do not support his/her recovery s/he needs other relationships with which to replace them. The client is most likely to find people quickly who will assist in his/her movement toward recovery within a 12-step program. Members of a 12-step program have firsthand experience with this dilemma and welcome contact with new members. Due to the emphasis on fellowship, clients usually have a much easier time forming relationships within 12-step programs than in most other groups. However, the pace and ability for the client to form relationships will vary greatly based on personality and characterological factors. How to integrate the relationships formed in 12-step programs with psychotherapy will be discussed in the next chapter.

The benefits of belonging to a group that is striving toward a common goal are recognized by the therapeutic community. 12-step programs are an excellent example of this principle. In addition to the individual relationships that are formed in 12-step programs, members also develop a sense of belonging to a group. At first the client bonds to specific meetings and eventually to the entire program. Members who identify with the program in general can go to any meeting and feel a sense of belonging. This can be especially beneficial when the member travels or moves to a new location.

Educating the client about the role and importance of building relationships within the 12-step program will assist the client in making this effort. Processing resistance is also important and will be discussed in the next chapter.

WORKING THE 12 STEPS

The phrase "working the 12 steps" usually refers to writing a response or history related to each step. Individual characteristics and situations determine when this process begins. The most important precursors are having a sponsor and regular, specific meeting attendance. Usually a member will be given direction from the sponsor on how to write a specific step, and most often will share this material with him/her. In addition, some steps can elicit strong emotions so having a support system in place is essential to preventing relapse into the addictive behavior. The role of the therapist is to understand the process of working the 12 steps as much as possible and to assist the client in exploring the emotions that surface in response to this work. Helping the client to write and share the response to each step is the role of the sponsor, not the therapist. Maintaining this balance can be delicate and requires close attention by the therapist.

It is helpful for therapists working with clients in 12-step programs to be familiar with what each step addresses. The steps can be divided into three sections. Steps One, Two, and Three focus on admitting the lack of control over addictive behavior and need for help to recover. Steps Four through Nine address the need for lifestyle and personality change, as well as taking responsibility for actions. Steps Ten, Eleven, and Twelve discuss the actions necessary to maintain recovery. Knowing what each step addresses can assist the therapist in responding to the emotions elicited by working that specific step. In addition it is also important for the clinician to know that clients in a structured outpatient program or residential setting will be encouraged to begin working the steps much sooner than those who are not.

INDIVIDUALITY IN THE PROGRAM

The most important role of the therapist is to help the client develop and maintain a sense of autonomy within the structure of a 12-step program. The need for autonomy will vary based on the level of ego development of the client. The stronger the internal locus of control, the greater the need for autonomy. It is important to assist the client in determining what will benefit him/her and what will not. There are several aspects of 12-step programs that all members are expected to accept without question. These include attending meetings, obtaining a sponsor, working the 12 steps, and developing a belief in a power greater than self. The culture of how and when these are implemented has developed over time, often resulting in pressure from certain members to do it in a proscribed manner rather than allowing for individual differences. Support for individuality in early recovery within the 12-step program is uncommon. Therefore, support for tailoring the program to meet the client's needs within the therapeutic alliance is essential.

For example, some 12-step programs strongly encourage new members to attend ninety meetings in ninety days. While this suggestion may be beneficial for clients who practiced their addictive behavior daily, those who acted out two or three times a week may not require daily support. A client who is able to abstain from the addictive behavior for several days at a time may resent the ninety meetings in ninety days suggestion. S/he will benefit from the therapist's support to determine the number of meetings which will help him/her abstain from the behavior completely. It is important for the therapist to be able to differentiate between individualizing a program and colluding with resistance. Therefore, if in doubt it is usually more helpful to encourage the client to try the 12-step program recommendation.

CONCLUSION

Educating the client about 12-step program involvement is a comprehensive process and may be quite lengthy. The clinician may devote the bulk of several sessions to assisting the client in bonding into the 12-step program. The benefits for the client and the therapist have been discussed in previous chapters. Once the groundwork has been laid for participation in a 12-step program, the therapist can begin to integrate the client's recovery process into psychotherapy, which is the subject of the next chapter.

6

Integrating 12-Step Principles and Treatment: Benefits and Difficulties

In order to work effectively with clients who can benefit from a 12-step program, the clinician needs to be able to integrate program principles into the therapeutic process, as well as identify and interpret potential difficulties inherent in this dynamic. This will differ somewhat depending on the therapist's theoretical orientation. These differences will be addressed throughout this chapter.

The most fundamental aspects of any therapeutic relationship are safety and confidentiality. A sense of safety develops in the therapeutic setting through the client's experience of the therapist as nonjudgmental and accepting, as well as knowledge of confidentiality. This same sense of safety evolves as the client witnesses these elements within the 12-step program. There is equal emphasis on confidentiality in all 12-step programs. One aspect of confidentiality, anonymity, is evidenced by the use of the word anonymous in the name of each program, and is clearly stated in Traditions Eleven and Twelve. The traditions of all 12-step programs state that no member will identify another member to anyone outside of the group, and will not share his/her own experience in any public forum, including the press. Another way in which safety can be experienced is in the lack of direct feedback to anything shared during a meeting. Therapists who work with a client in 12-step programs can help him/her identify and articulate his/her reaction about belonging to a group where s/he feels safe to talk about him/herself, sometimes for the first time in his/her life.

It is also important to recognize that some clients may not experience this feeling of safety. Part of the task for the therapist is to distinguish between external and internal safety issues. For example, are there members of a specific meeting who are violating confidentiality, or is the client unable to recognize a safe environment?

The primary ways 12-step programs enhance the therapeutic process include:

1. Expanding the support system
2. Providing a place to learn and practice new coping skills
3. Motivating and opening members to change as a process
4. Promoting personal responsibility
5. Learning about and understanding differences
6. Having a common language

Some of the difficulties that may arise include: splitting between the therapist and the sponsor or others in the 12-step program, distorting program philosophy, distinguishing between empowerment and surrender, and negotiating the reality of multiple helpers. The manner in which the benefits and problems are manifested will vary depending on the client's stage of recovery, as well as his/her ability to bond, degree of concrete or abstract thinking, capacity to self-soothe, capacity for awareness or insight, history of interpersonal relationships, and the presence of any biochemical psychiatric disorder.

All of the material in this chapter rests on the premise that psychotherapy with a client in a 12-step program is a collaborative process. The therapist's role is often that of a guide and a member of a treatment team that communicates through the client, especially in early recovery. Some theoretical approaches may have more difficulty with this premise than others. In some respects this is unique; in other ways it is similar to the client who has a strong relationship with a mentor/teacher or his/her religious organization. The client may receive guidance from his/her teacher or clergyperson about issues also discussed with the therapist. This is not usually viewed as problematic, nor does the therapist usually discourage the client from such discussions. It does however need to be integrated into the therapeutic relationship. It is important for the therapist to value the process the client is having in the 12-step program, just as the therapist would honor the significance of the client's relationship with his/her mentor/teacher or church. Clients well into the recovery process are more able to tolerate ambiguity between the therapist and his/her 12-step support system.

In addition to working from the collaborative model, the client's stage of recovery greatly impacts how the clinician integrates the therapeutic process with the 12-step experience. Many perspectives identify three stages of recovery: Early, Middle, and Late. Early Recovery is generally thought of as the period of time when the client identifies his/her addiction, and initiates the lifestyle changes necessary to abstain from that addiction. This is also the time when the client begins to develop new coping mechanisms, learn about the 12-step program, and build a new support system. How these goals are accomplished will vary according to theoretical orientation. Early Recovery usually lasts from one to two years and is focused on external changes, while Middle Recovery emphasizes internal change. The major tasks of Middle Recovery include identifying and working through personality and cognitive style, family of origin, and current interpersonal relationship issues. This process often lasts several years. The length of this stage is usually determined by the ability of the client to embrace and integrate change. In Late Recovery the client has developed the ability to maintain the changes already accomplished, and continue to grow in response to life situations. Some members never reach Late Recovery. Factors which may contribute to the lack of progress beyond Middle Recovery include personality disorders, extreme anxiety, other psychiatric disorders such as schizophrenia, and/or lack of insight. One of the reasons for supporting 12-step program attendance for people in Late Recovery is the recognition of growth as a lifelong process.

EXPANDING THE SUPPORT SYSTEM

One of the primary benefits of integrating 12-step principles into therapy is the support system the 12-step program establishes. As discussed in chapter 5, in the section on rationale, most clients with an addiction require more support than the therapist can provide. This need for support evolves over time from dependence to healthy interdependence as the client progresses in recovery. Clients in Early Recovery usually require a higher degree of dependence on both the therapist and the 12-step program. This evolves into healthy interdependence as the client progresses in therapy and moves into the later stages of recovery. One benefit of integrating 12-step involvement in the therapeutic process, as previously discussed, is that the therapist is not the sole provider of support in this person's life. An example is the case of a client with very high dependency needs and a history of suicidal behavior who called her therapist two to three times a week between sessions. Once she began participation in a 12-step program, the therapist was able to gradually help her build a support system outside of therapy and the calls between sessions were reduced to one every three or four weeks. Knowing the client had other people in her support network allowed the therapist to set firmer limits without fear of the client acting out in a destructive manner.

A client-centered therapist would conceptualize this extended support system as providing additional opportunities for the client to experience unconditional positive regard, empathy, and genuineness. Increasing the number of relationships in which these elements exist assists the client in building trust and integrating these qualities into his/her life. Additionally, the therapist has more material to use in the therapeutic setting to reinforce the development of a new self image. Given the universal acceptance of these concepts, most therapists, regardless of theoretical orientation, recognize the importance of these experiences for any client.

Therapists who work from a psychodynamic framework would describe the support system provided by 12-step programs as extending the holding environment. It is generally accepted that time, place, money, and the relationship are some of the elements of the therapeutic holding environment. In keeping with this approach, each specific meeting is held at the same time and place every week, and each member is asked to donate what s/he can afford at the end of these meetings. Relationships are an integral part of any 12-step program and exist on several levels. The client has individual relationships with other members including his/her sponsor, with specific meetings attended on a regular basis, and with the program as a whole.

In the holding environment provided by a 12-step program, the client has increased opportunities for positive mirroring, a place to practice new behaviors in an accepting culture, as well as additional structure. One of the ways a client may experience positive mirroring in the 12-step program is in the nonverbal responses from other members when s/he shares in a meeting. This might be nodding, smiling, or making eye contact. The therapist who is familiar with 12-step programs will assist the client in becoming more aware of these responses and to be able to internalize them.

Another psychodynamic concept is the process by which clients attain object constancy. The first step in this journey is to form an attachment with a primary love object. In most cases the therapist becomes the object. However, clients who are bonded into a 12-step program prior to beginning therapy will use the program as the primary attachment figure. It is essential that the therapist recognize, respect, and support this connection. If the therapist attempts to prematurely shift the client's primary attachment object, it is likely the client will abort therapy in service of keeping the primary relationship.

Another step in the process of attaining object constancy is the development and use of transitional objects. Clients in 12-step programs may use aspects of the program, such as phone contact with other members, as transitional objects as they learn to self-soothe. Therapists who recognize this concept will support the client in attending meetings as often as needed during this stage of development. Frequent contact with the sponsor or other members of the program may also serve this function. Therapists working from this model will encourage clients to reach out to other program members, either in person or by telephone, when they are in distress.

Behaviorist clinicians study the conditions necessary for change and believe that part of the problem is the current environment in which the client functions. 12-step programs provide a new environment which sets up new conditions for learning. An important function of the therapist is modeling new behavior. Attending meetings, as well as other interactions with program members, gives clients additional opportunities to learn through observation and modeling. Cognitive-behaviorists also believe that changing distorted cognitions is one of the primary methods of achieving behavior change. Irrational beliefs related to the addictive process are often confronted and disputed in relationships with other 12-step program members. All of the above conditions for change are enhanced by expanding the client's 12-step program support system.

Gestalt therapists maintain that contact is essential for change and growth to occur. Consequently group therapy is a frequently used modality in gestalt work. While 12-step programs are not facilitated groups, many of the dynamics are similar. Sharing in the here-and-now, feeling accepted by a group, and increased contact with self can be part of the 12-step process. All of these elements need to be experienced, and integrating 12-step participation into the therapeutic realm expands the client's potential for growth. This external support system gradually evolves into an internalized experience.

Reality therapy believes that all behaviors are an attempt to meet one's needs. The experience of love and belonging is one of these essential needs. Expanding the places in which a client may discover these feelings can be facilitated by involvement in a 12-step program. This provides an additional place for the client to explore the difference between his/her internal and external reality. All 12-step programs state that the only requirement for membership, and thus acceptance as part of the group, is identification of and desire to change an addiction. Therefore, most clients will have the experience of belonging to a group when they become involved in a 12-step program. Feeling loved is the result of developing individual relationships within the program and thus takes more time. Reality therapists will recognize the value of expanding the supportive environment in which the client may explore the distinction between his/her internal and external reality.

One of the central tenets of existential therapy is how a sense of alienation and isolation contributes to emotional distress. All clients with an addictive process have some degree of isolation and sense of alienation. Belonging to a group of people with a common problem can reduce both of these conditions. Existential therapy focuses on the relationship between the therapist and the client, and emphasizes authenticity. 12-step programs support this dynamic by encouraging authentic interactions among members at both a group and individual level. Integration of 12-step program involvement into the therapeutic process can facilitate the development of authenticity, and decrease isolation and alienation. The existential therapist may use interactions the client describes with both individuals and in meetings to assist the client in identifying meaningful interpersonal experiences.

The concept of looking at the system to bring about individual change is central to family systems theory. Beginning 12-step program participation enables the client to enter a new, and potentially healthier, system. Assisting the client to identify his/her role in both the original and new systems is an integral part of this therapy. One of the therapeutic tasks can be helping the client interact in the new system differently than s/he did in his/her original system. One of the newer systems theories, narrative therapy, emphasizes the importance of finding an audience/system for the client's new story. 12-step meetings can provide such an audience for the client to process in therapy.

The various theories may differ in how to utilize and integrate the expanded support system; however, they all value its importance. Everything in the discussion above applies to any stage of the recovery process. However, there are some issues specific to each stage. The following identifies issues related to expanding the support system in each stage of recovery.

Early Recovery

Expanding the support system is one of the largest areas of concern for both the therapist and the client in Early Recovery. Most people with an addictive process are either isolative or have relationships which center around the addiction. Therefore, one of the major tasks of Early Recovery is the development of relationships which support the recovery process. The therapist's role in this task may be to encourage the client to assess and develop new relationships, teach the skills needed to develop and participate in new relationships, and/or assist the client in assessing existing relationships.

In Early Recovery, the therapist will be more actively involved in helping the client with external structure. As stated earlier, most clients in this stage require more external support than the therapist can provide. 12-step meetings, as well as individual interactions with the sponsor and other members, can provide part of the client's external support system outside of the therapeutic setting.

Although there are many benefits to a client in Early Recovery having this support system, there are also difficulties. The majority of these problems are centered around splitting between the therapist and the 12-step program. This occurs when conflicting information or suggestions are given. The client may obtain these from his/her sponsor, in a meeting, or in an individual discussion with another member. Clients in Early Recovery have much less ability to tolerate and process conflicting positions between those perceived as helpers. Clients in this stage are not well individuated, have many distorted cognitions, want and often actually need more direction and, therefore, frequently look for external answers. When those answers are different, clients in Early Recovery have difficulty knowing what to do with that information. It is wise for therapists working with these clients to anticipate and address this phenomenon. The issues that will arise are partially dependent upon whether the client's initial bond is with the therapist or the 12-step program.

If the client began therapy prior to starting 12-step program involvement, it is likely that the primary bond will be with the therapist. In this case, the therapist is more able to disagree with the 12-step program position without threatening the therapeutic alliance. When the primary bond is with the 12-step program the therapist must be more careful in processing any difference of opinion. How the therapist addresses these conflicts will vary depending on the therapist's style and the client's ability to tolerate ambiguity. A specific difference of opinion can arise when clients in Early Recovery receive a message from some members that the 12-step program can serve the same function as therapy. It is important for the therapist to dispute this particular message and clearly identify the difference between what therapy and the 12-step program can provide.

Middle Recovery

A client in Middle Recovery beginning psychotherapy will have experienced the benefit and necessity of the expanded support system. Splitting may again pose a problem; however, the client in this stage has usually developed an increased ability to process different information and suggestions. These clients have already had several experiences receiving divergent opinions on topics. The therapist needs to understand and respect that the client has a strong bond with the 12-step program. The development of the therapeutic alliance may take longer, and although the client may have more tolerance for differences of opinion, conflicting positions will need to be addressed more carefully.

Late Recovery

Clients who begin psychotherapy while in the later stage of recovery will have a support system firmly in place. By definition a client is not considered in late recovery unless s/he has worked through enough issues to be able to establish and maintain intimate relationships. One of the therapeutic tasks may be assisting the client in expanding this support system outside of the 12-step program. All of the skills the client learned in the 12-step program will assist him/her in forming relationships outside of the program. The focus of therapy for this client will more likely be related to life transition issues, and will thus focus primarily on the presenting problem.

PLACE TO LEARN AND PRACTICE NEW COPING SKILLS

The idea of a place to practice new behaviors is common to psychodynamic, cognitive-behavioral, reality, family systems, and gestalt therapy. These modalities include developing a new way of interrelating. 12-step programs reinforce this concept and give the client multiple opportunities in a safe environment to experiment with new ways of interacting. Regardless of theoretical orientation, therapists can assist clients in practicing new behaviors by processing his/her reactions to program experiences in therapy sessions. Psychodynamic therapists may focus on the client's projections, cognitive-behaviorists on distorted cognitions or beliefs, gestalt therapists on the here and now rather than the past, family systems therapists on how to interact with a new system, and reality therapists on how the five essential needs are being met. No matter what the focus, the process is the same. The client has an experience in the 12-step program related to a behavior s/he is learning, and discusses that experience with the therapist in order to understand what worked and what needs adjusting. This process is repeated many times as the client integrates a new behavior into his/her life. As the client moves through the stages of recovery, the specific behaviors and coping skills targeted will change.

Early Recovery

The focus in Early Recovery is on concrete, behavioral change. The role of the therapist in this stage is primarily psychoeducational in nature. Consequently, the therapist is often more directive than with clients further along in the recovery process. Clients in early recovery learn through observation and imitation rather than through integration and emotional insight. There are two major ways that clients become aware of behaviors they need to change or learn. The therapist or another member of the 12-step program, often the sponsor, may ask the client how s/he is handling particular situations. The other way a client may become aware of needed behavior change is through being in situations where s/he becomes uncomfortable with and/or unable to deal with the situation. Once the therapist and the client identify a behavior that needs to be changed or learned, the 12-step meetings can provide a place where clients will hear about and observe behaviors utilized successfully by members in later stages of recovery. The therapist can then discuss or process with the client how s/he can adopt the new behavior.

For example, how do clients learn to avoid places where the addiction is practiced, or cope with being in places s/he is unable to avoid where addictive behavior is present? In the case of a client with an eating disorder, it is impossible to avoid situations entirely where large amounts of food are available. Therefore, one of the tasks in Early Recovery is learning how to eat in places where larger portions are served and/or available. The therapist can assist the client in gathering information about how other 12-step program members address these types of situations, and then assist the client in choosing the alternative that best suits him/her. Part of the therapeutic interaction will probably include some form of direction or psychoeducation in this example. A client may distort or misinterpret the suggestions made by other 12-step program members. If a client proposes a solution that seems fed by the addiction, it is helpful for the therapist to point this out. Continuing with the above example, the client may come up with a solution of only going to buffet-style restaurants thinking s/he will be able to determine the portion size, when in fact, this solution may be prompted by eating-disorder-thinking related to avoiding any restriction of food choices or amounts available. Most eating-disorder clients in Early Recovery are unable to judge appropriate portion size. The therapist's role here is to point out the addictive thinking and assist the client in finding a more appropriate solution.

Perhaps the most essential task in Early Recovery is developing the ability to identify and articulate one's needs and emotions. Helping clients in this process is imperative and can be a major focus in therapy. Furthermore, developing coping skills to handle the emerging feelings is facilitated and supported in both the therapeutic setting and 12-step program involvement. As the major purpose of any addiction is to alter mood, helping the client identify and build tolerance for affective responses is a large part of the entire recovery process. Changing addictive behaviors is not enough for quality recovery. For example, the alcoholic who has been sober for ten years and is still filled with unexpressed rage and lashing out inappropriately is not an example of the kind of recovery for which to strive. The person may have stopped the addictive use of alcohol and changed behaviors directly related to drinking, but s/he may not have learned to identify and cope with emotions effectively.

The major coping skills suggested in 12-step programs include sharing in meetings, talking with other members outside of meetings, especially the sponsor, writing about feelings, reading program literature, meditating or praying, and learning relaxation techniques. Most theoretical modalities support many, if not all, of these interventions. In addition, the therapist may use role plays, guided imagery, identification of body sensations, bibliotherapy, or the therapeutic relationship to assist the client in this process.

Another important element in Early Recovery is learning basic communication skills. Although this will be a major part of the therapeutic process, the client will have more opportunities during the week to practice these new skills interacting with 12-step program members than with the therapist. The role of the therapist is to aid the client in identifying people and/or situations where communication is impaired or difficult. Then the therapist helps the client learn new ways of communicating. For example, this may be as simple as helping a client make statements such as "No, I don't want to go out to a bar tonight." or "I'm not ready to see a movie with explicit sexual scenes." The therapist will need to assess the client's ability to communicate in order to know where to begin. Some clients with an addiction have not learned the ability to make rudimentary, direct self-statements and thus must begin at an elementary level.

Also in Early Recovery, clients must learn to replace old activities related to the addiction with new, healthier actions. The initial activity used to replace addictive behaviors is attendance at 12-step program meetings. As described in previous chapters, this may be attending ninety meetings in ninety days or a similar plan. Once the client has begun to abstain from addictive behavior, the therapist can help him/her explore other interests such as time spent with family or friends, athletic or recreational activities, a hobby, or beginning classes.

Middle Recovery

In Early Recovery the focus is on introducing and learning new behaviors. In Middle Recovery it is integrating the new coping skills into personality style. Clients shift from learning new behaviors simply by observation and imitation, to utilizing internal awareness as a tool. Although the client will continue to learn and practice new coping mechanisms within the context of the therapeutic setting and 12-step programs, the focus will shift from elementary skills to more advanced abilities, as well as reinforcement of those previously learned. This is also where the client begins to fine tune and integrate these elements into his/her lifestyle.

By now the client has learned to identify and articulate emotions, as well as learned basic communications skills. Therapists will be able to help a client who began psychotherapy during Early Recovery transition into learning more advanced communication skills such as accurate empathy and matching verbal and nonverbal messages.

Therapists who begin work with a client in Middle Recovery will need to do an in-depth assessment of the client's communication capabilities in order to develop an appropriate treatment plan. It is during this stage of recovery that clients learn to discharge feelings at a deeper level. An essential part of the role of the therapist is to determine the client's ability to tolerate and express various intensities of affect appropriately and safely. One of the important aspects of this process is developing skills that allow the client to satisfy his/her needs without violating others. The single most effective way to demonstrate this ability is in advanced communication methods of distinguishing between, and articulating effectively, needs and wants.

An example of this is a story told by a famous speaker in AA and ACA. His current wife became very ill. His previous wife had died of cancer several years before. His current wife stated she did not feel that he was emotionally supportive of her during her illness. He was confused by this statement as he had made her meals and changed her bed. When she confronted him, he searched internally and admitted he was not able to be present emotionally in the way she needed due to his unresolved grief about his previous wife's death. He was able to say that he wanted to be present but knew he could not do so, and suggested that she seek this need from others. This is an example of both advanced communication skills and the ability to identify and articulate emotions.

Late Recovery

The transition between Middle and Late Recovery is characterized by a decreased dependence on 12-step program participation alone. A client in Late Recovery needs to have many places to learn and practice new coping skills. The challenge now is adapting these skills to a variety of situations. The focus of therapy with someone in Late Recovery will be dealing with more subtle issues or life transitions not previously experienced. This may entail expanding the arenas in which the client may interact and practice new behaviors. For example, a client dealing with a dying parent may attend a hospice support group, in addition to 12-step program involvement and therapy. A heterosexual client who desires a healthy, sexual relationship may choose to work with an opposite-sex therapist with whom s/he is attracted in order to change the pattern of relating in an intimate relationship. The 12-step program may then become one of the places where the client practices new behaviors and new ways of relating; however, the original learning takes place in the therapeutic relationship. Therefore, one of the hallmarks of Late Recovery is the shift from primarily relying on 12-step program involvement as the place to practice new behaviors. The client in Late Recovery learns and incorporates new behaviors from a multitude of sources.

MOTIVATION AND OPENNESS TO CHANGE

One of the primary assumptions in both psychotherapy and membership in a 12-step program is the desire for some form of personal change. Equally important is the examination of all aspects of personality and how one interacts with the world. Clients who have just realized the impact of their addiction are often the most motivated to change. They usually experience a sense of desperation and willingness to try almost anything which can enhance the therapeutic process. The therapist can assume that all clients involved in a 12-step program will be repeatedly advised to take a deep look at the self as evidenced by Steps Four through Nine. The member is encouraged to take a detailed look at his/her behavior and the consequences for self and others. This is most evident in Steps Four and Five, where the member is asked to do an inventory of actions and feelings that have caused problems in his/her life. The next step is to share those with another person. Whether the formal sharing is done with the therapist or another member, therapy can be very helpful in this process of self-examination. When the member is clearly seeing the problems the addiction has caused in his/her life the motivation for change usually increases. Steps Six and Seven require the member to become willing to change "defects of character" and ask for help in this process. The focus of Steps Eight and Nine is to make amends for behavior harmful to self and others.

Another benefit of working with a client in recovery is that 12-step programs promote the concept that change takes time, and growth is a life-long process. This is most strongly evidenced by the emphasis on staying in the program for life. Many therapists may or may not subscribe to this belief. It is important that the therapist not impose his/her opinion about the length of 12-step program involvement on the client. The period of time a client may benefit from this kind of support needs to be assessed on an individual basis. Things to be considered include the development of an internal locus of control, object constancy, a strong support system outside the 12-step program, and the client's desire to stay involved or discontinue membership.

A strength of 12-step programs is the opportunity to observe members who are further along in the recovery process and are still motivated to change. In a healthy 12-step meeting, there is a core group of members who have both stopped the addictive behavior and incorporated the principles of the program into their daily living. Clients who attend such meetings have role models who demonstrate the benefit of commitment to long-term self-examination and change. This culture of change provides an extension of the holding environment and usually enhances the therapeutic process. One of the responsibilities of the therapist is to assist the client in finding and identifying healthy meetings. Some of the aspects the therapist will want to discuss include: what factors make up a healthy meeting, how to evaluate who is a healthy sponsor, how to determine which behaviors to incorporate, and how to use the therapeutic process to enhance the 12-step experience. As discussed in chapter 5, the important elements of a healthy meeting include: discussion of feelings as well as behaviors, acceptance of the relationship between past experiences and development of the addiction, the presence of several members with more than five years in recovery, sharing of individual differences respectfully, and minimal disruptions due to members moving about the room.

Early Recovery

Clients who have just realized the impact of their addictive behavior are the most desperate and open to change. This is a window of opportunity the therapist can utilize. The major focus in this stage is usually on external behavioral changes. There is a small percentage of clients who, upon stopping the addictive behavior, have family-of-origin or PTSD issues which surface immediately and thus must be addressed for them to be able to keep the behavior in remission. The therapeutic task is to carefully assess whether the client needs to address these issues or is using them as a smoke screen to avoid dealing with the consequences of the addiction.

When a client is in Early Recovery, there are a significant number of external changes that need to occur. The task of the therapist is to assist the client in determining which behaviors take precedence. During this process the therapist will need to be more directive and cognitive-behaviorally focused than in later stages of recovery. There are some similarities to crisis intervention counseling; however, the significant difference is the higher degree of therapeutic alliance needed by the addicted client.

Middle Recovery

The client in therapy at this stage experiences a less desperate need for change. By this time, the belief that growth is a lifelong process should be incorporated by the client. However, the client's characterological issues and resistance to change will be more apparent. The focus of therapy shifts to internal rather than external change and thus may occur more slowly. The therapist, depending on theorectial orientation and personal style, will be less directive. This may be disconcerting to the client who has been in directive therapy while in Early Recovery, whether with the same clinician or beginning with someone new.

One way the therapist will know the shift needs to occur is when the client begins resisting direction previously desired. The client will begin to voice a need for more autonomy and will demonstrate the ability to problem-solve and identify emotions and distorted cognitions. It is essential that the therapist follow the client's lead in this process. Another sign the client is ready for this change is the emergence of relational or family-of-origin issues as the dominant focus of therapy.

If a therapist begins to see a client in this stage, who was in counseling at some point in early recovery, a transition still needs to be accomplished. The dynamics will be different as a new relationship is being formed rather than changing an existing one.

Late Recovery

One of the hallmarks of Late versus Middle Recovery is that the characterological issues and resistance to change have been identified and partially resolved. Consequently, a client entering therapy in this stage demonstrates a greater openness to change without the desperation of Early Recovery. The commitment to lifelong growth is fully integrated.

PROMOTION OF PERSONAL RESPONSIBILITY

The development and acceptance of personal responsibility is an integral part of any psychotherapy. This is also an essential aspect of all 12-step programs. Personal responsibility permeates the entire 12-step philosophy. Steps Six and Seven advise members to begin the process of personality change which implies taking responsibility for it. Furthermore, Steps Eight and Nine reinforce the need for personal responsibility by suggesting the member make direct amends for any harmful behavior. Step Ten encourages the continuation of this process for the rest of the member's life. These elements can support and accelerate the therapeutic process.

Clients with an addictive process often vacillate between taking no responsibility or total responsibility for events in their lives. An essential aspect of therapy is assisting the client to identify actual responsibility as it applies to various situations. One of the ways clients may unconsciously avoid examining their behavior is by repeatedly creating or actively contributing to the development of life crises. As with any client, this process must be addressed therapeutically.

Early Recovery

One of the most important aspects of Early Recovery is learning to take personal responsibility for past and present behavior. As stated earlier, this stage focuses on external change. The philosophy of the program is that external change leads to internal change. This is a position held by some theoretical orientations as well. An integral part of change becoming internal is the acceptance of appropriate responsibility. The role of the therapist with the client in Early Recovery is to facilitate this process while modulating self-blame. This process can often be difficult and frustrating for both the client and the therapist.

Middle Recovery

A significant hallmark of the transition to Middle Recovery is the integration of the ability to identify and acknowledge personal responsibility in many different situations. Working with these clients is often rewarding due to their willingness to examine various aspects of internal and interpersonal issues. Any resistance the therapist observes is more likely to be characterological and a defense against shame. The approach with these clients is usually the same as with nonaddictive clients who enter therapy to address deeper issues.

Late Recovery

There is no significant difference in this area between clients well into Middle Recovery and those in Late Recovery.

LEARNING ABOUT AND UNDERSTANDING DIFFERENCES

Identifying and accepting differences are two of the most complex and difficult processes in human development. The ability to understand differences comes from self-acceptance. People with an addictive process have poor self-esteem and struggle with self-acceptance which can interfere with the development of tolerance and understanding. The capacity to empathetically understand another person's life experience develops from the concrete recognition of the existence of differences in the latency-age child into the mature, abstract understanding of the adult regarding the impact of those differences. For example, the latency-age child perceives the concrete fact that two people have different skin color. The mature adult also perceives this difference and has an empathic understanding of its meaning. In addition, s/he acknowledges the inability to truly comprehend the other person's experience and the impact on his/her life. So a mature adult who relates to a person of a different ethnic background is able to admit s/he does not have the same life experience and thus may empathize with, but cannot fully know, the other's experience.

12-step programs foster the acceptance of differences in a variety of ways. One of the most obvious is that anyone is accepted into the program who has a desire to stop the addictive behavior. This implies tolerance of all differences regarding race, gender, age, sexual orientation, religion, political affiliation, or any other category. Another example is the "no cross-talk" rule. One of the purposes of this rule is to prevent members from making comments which might be perceived as intolerance. Consequently, people hear a variety of perspectives and begin to understand and integrate the value of these differences. This process may begin with hearing concretely different methods members have used to abstain from the addictive behavior, including many abstract ways of defining "Higher Power," and developing into mature appreciation for the richness available from interacting with widely diverse members.

One of the strengths of 12-step programs is the acceptance of diverse definitions of spirituality. This tolerance for difference is also an important part of learning acceptance of self and others. Although there are specific guidelines regarding the process of recovery, 12-step programs are known for tolerating significant differences in how one achieves that recovery. For example, one member will begin to "work" the 12 steps within the first three months of entering a program, while another will wait one year before beginning that process. While some members may have an opinion about which way is preferable, as long as the member is abstaining from the addiction, each way is accepted.

The degree of diversity varies greatly among categories of addiction. AA and NA are the most diverse of all the programs. This is partly due to the fact that the use of mood-altering substances is universal. Racial background is the category less represented in the other 12-step programs. However, a multitude of other differences exist and acceptance of them is promoted in all programs. The mere fact the member identifies him/herself as part of a group with such diverse membership facilitates the development of tolerance and understanding.

Early Recovery

In the very beginning the clinician wants the client to attend a homogenous rather than heterogeneous group, in order to facilitate identification with the program. It is easier for human beings to identify with people more similar than not. Therefore, it is not a goal in very Early Recovery to help the client appreciate differences. As the person begins to abstain from the addictive behavior and identifies strongly with the group, the tolerance for differences begins to develop. As stated earlier, this process begins with the concrete and gradually matures. By the time the member is beginning the transition to Middle Recovery this process should have begun.

Middle Recovery

The person in Middle Recovery has usually developed the ability to accept, or at least tolerate, differences. The capacity to empathetically understand the significance of these differences is based on the individual's ability to connect and think abstractly. Those members who have impairment in these areas will have greater difficulty accepting differences, and will seek meetings which are more homogenous in nature. It is a clinical judgment when to encourage a client to attend more heterogeneous meetings based on these capacities. Some clients may never move beyond Middle Recovery.

Late Recovery

The client in Late Recovery has the capacity to understand and embrace differences. S/he has experienced the richness inherent in relating to people with vastly different life experiences. Membership in a 12-step program gives the therapist a useful tool to assist the client in the process of valuing diversity.

HAVING A COMMON LANGUAGE

The capacity to communicate is rooted in language. A common language is one of the most fundamental ways in which a person identifies him/herself as part of a group. One of the components which creates cohesion in a group is the development of phrases and terms unique to that group. 12-step programs have many common phrases which have their own unique meaning. The initial purpose of these phrases is to give the member small concrete tools to guide him/her through what can otherwise be an overwhelming process. The program sayings are similar to mantras or road signs. Just as the signs tell us when to stop, when to go, when to yield or slow down, program sayings such as "one day at a time," "easy does it," or "first things first" can help navigate the road to recovery.

These phrases may also serve as transitional objects which help the client self-soothe. For example, when a client is having an urge to act out an addictive behavior, the phrase "one day at a time" can help him/her refrain from the behavior just for that day or even that minute. The phrase becomes linked with many corrective emotional experiences and cognitive reframes. This can be a very useful therapeutic intervention when the clinician uses the phrase to elicit the link, as well as an effective way to integrate the 12-step program into the therapeutic process.

Application of the meaning of these phrases is generalized beyond the addictive behaviors as the person progresses in recovery. For example, a client whose spouse is ill might use the phrase "one day at a time" to cope with the fear and sadness related to the possibility of losing his/her partner. The therapist who knows the program sayings can use them with the client and thus elicit the responses associated with them. It is very similar to the client who has had a difficult situation arise and asked him/herself, "What would my therapist say/do?" The client is beginning to internalize the therapist and use him/her outside of the therapeutic environment in the client's world. This same process occurs in the 12-step program.

CONCLUSION

Integrating psychotherapy and 12-step program involvement is complex. Factors such as the client's stage of recovery, psychological development, and spiritual belief system, as well as negotiating the reality of multiple helpers, all impact this integration. The client is best served when the clinician has an understanding of, and appreciation for, the value of the 12-step program, and is able to utilize its principles to enhance the therapeutic process. The way the therapist integrates these principles will vary based on theoretical orientation and assessment of the client. Utilizing both psychotherapy and 12-step program support assists the client in moving through the process of recovery with greater depth and speed.

Appendix A: Glossary

TERMS

Anonymity: Concept that an essential aspect of any 12-step program meeting being a safe place is members knowing his/her identity will be protected by all other members. No member will reveal another member's name to a nonmember.

Big Book: This term usually refers to the book *Alcoholics Anonymous*. Many of the newer 12-step programs use this book and change "alcohol" to the addictive behavior addressed by that program. For example, Sex and Love Addicts Anonymous members would change "alcohol" to "sexually compulsive behavior" or "addictive relationships."

"Bottom Line Behavior:" Used primarily in programs which address behaviors which the member will continue but in moderation. For example, sex addicts will have a "bottom line" number of times they may have sexual activity in a day or a week. Any activity in excess of this amount will be considered addictive.

Committed Step Studies: Step study meetings where members form a group which goes through all 12 steps together.

These meetings are not published on any meeting schedule and become closed to any new members after the first two to four weeks.

Cross Addiction: The belief that an alcoholic or drug addict who uses a different mood-altering substance than the one(s) to which s/he was originally addicted will either become addicted to the new substance or relapse with the original one. It is an integral part of the rationale for all alcoholics/drug addicts to abstain from all mood-altering substances.

Denial: Defense mechanism common to all people with any kind of addictive process. It may develop over time or be present prior to beginning the addictive behavior.

Disease: Theory that addictive behavior, particularly chemical dependency, has a genetic or biological aspect. Foundation of the medical model approach to treatment.

Drug of Choice: Refers to the substance preferred by the addict regardless of how many different types of drugs the person may use.

Fellowship: Relationships with other members of the 12-step program. Usually used to describe the experience of belonging to the group, rather than individual relationships.

Half-measures: Attempts to change which are incomplete or do not include what is difficult.

High Bottom: Person who began his/her recovery process before the addictive behavior caused moderate or severe consequences. For example, a compulsive gambler who stopped gambling before losing his/her marriage or life savings.

Hitting Bottom: Emotional experience when the consequences of the addiction breaks through the client's denial system. Usually results in the person seeking help. However, the denial system may reconstitute and the opportunity for recovery may pass.

Home Group: Meeting the member identifies as the primary support group and which s/he usually attends every week.

Insanity: Doing the same thing over and over and expecting different results.

Inventory: List of behaviors member sees in self or others needing change. This is a positive thing when applied to self and negative when done to others.

Message: Teachings of the 12-step program, especially that recovery is possible.

Miracle: Being able to abstain from the addictive behavior and experience the benefits of applying the program philosophy to life.

Normies: People without any addictive behavior, especially the behavior targeted by the program to which the member belongs. Nonalcoholics, even if they have an eating disorder, are "normies" to members of AA.

Relapse: Returning to addictive behavior after a period of time of abstaining.

Service: Time devoted to working with other members of the program or performing a task for a meeting or larger group. Examples include being a sponsor, secretary of a meeting, inter-group representative, or making coffee.

Sharing/Discussion Meetings: Meetings where members talk about personal experiences usually related to a specific topic.

Slip: Reverting to addictive behavior, usually for a short period of time.

Speaker Meetings: Meetings where one or more members, usually with a significant period of recovery, share their personal stories about the development of their addiction, and how they attained recovery.

Sponsor: Person with whom the member works individually. The primary purpose of the sponsor is to guide the member throughout the 12 steps. However, most members consult their sponsor on a wide range of decisions and issues.

Step-Study Meetings: Meetings which focus on the 12 steps. Usually one step is discussed each week. These meetings are open to anyone in the program, are published in the meeting schedule, and members can begin attending the meeting at any point in the 12 step cycle, unlike committed step studies.

Token: A concrete symbol of periods of time in recovery. Tokens are usually key chains for three-, six-, and nine-month segments and a specially made coin for year anniversaries.

Twelve Steps: The heart of the program philosophy. See chapter 1 for a complete list and description.

Twelve Traditions: Ways the program functions. See chapter 1 for a complete list and description.

We Agnostics: An officially recognized branch of AA which benefits from AA's central organization. The basic AA approach is interpreted without the religious components.

Working the Steps: Process of applying the 12 steps to an individual member. This usually involves the member writing an individual response to each step and sharing it with the sponsor.

PHRASES

Do the Footwork and Leave the Results Up to God: The member is responsible for actions but is not in control of end result, "God" is.

Easy Does It: Don't overreact to life events. Stress and excessive emotion can lead to relapse so should be avoided as much as possible.

Fake It Til You Make It: Pretend things are better, or that the member believes part of the program philosophy, until it becomes true for the person.

F.E.A.R.: False evidence appearing real.

The First Drink Gets You Drunk: 12-step programs believe the addicted person loses control of the addictive behavior once it is resumed. This is particularly true in chemical dependency, but applies to all programs.

First Things First: Actions or decisions which are necessary to attain and maintain recovery are seen as more important than anything else. 12-step programs teach that recovery comes before all other aspects of a person's life.

H.A.L.T.: Hungry, angry, lonely, and/or tired. Members are advised to avoid any of these states.

H.O.W.: Honesty, open-mindedness, and willingness. Members are encouraged to develop these characteristics.

Keep Coming Back, It Works: Encouragement to continue attending meetings because the program will prove helpful over time.

K.I.S.S.: Keep it simple, stupid. People with addictive behaviors often make things more complicated than necessary. This phrase reminds members to simplify their lives.

Live and Let Live: Tolerance for others is an important aspect of all 12-step programs.

Living Life on Life's Terms: Accepting reality without trying to change or manipulate the results is a key aspect to program philosophy.

Misery Is Optional: Part of the cognitive aspect of 12-step programs. The concepts that members can choose their feelings by examining and changing their thought patterns, thus feeling bad is a choice.

My Worst Day Sober Was Better than My Best Day Drunk: Addresses how life improves once the addictive behavior is in remission.

One Day at a Time: Emphasizes the program philosophy to live in the present. The member only needs to abstain from the addictive behavior today. However, this does not mean to refrain from having goals, just that tomorrow cannot be predicted.

One Drink Is Too Many and a Thousand Isn't Enough: Reinforces the concept that alcoholics cannot drink any alcohol.

Praying Only for "His" Will and the Power to Carry It Out: The member is encouraged to ask for guidance from his/her "Higher Power," whatever that is, and the ability to implement the guidance received.

Progress Not Perfection: All that is expected is that the member address and make progress changing problematic behaviors and attitudes. It is especially understood that no one can apply the 12 steps to life completely or at all times.

Self-will Run Riot: The member's inability to accept suggestions or directions. The person exhibits a desire to do things his/her way regardless of past experience.

Stinking Thinking: Thought patterns which cause trouble for the member. Often contains some form of denial.

Surrender: Ability to accept lack of control. Usually implies an emotional experience as well as cognitive pattern.

Today Is the First Day of the Rest of Your Life: Emphasizes the concept of living in the present and letting go of the past.

You Can't Keep It Unless You Give It Away: An important element of recovery is contributing to others. This slogan states each member has to be engaged in service to keep his/her own recovery process intact.

Appendix B: Prayers Commonly Used in 12-Step Programs

Eleventh Step Prayer: "Lord, make me a channel of the peace—that where there is hatred, I may bring love—that where there is wrong, I may bring the spirit of forgiveness—that where there is discord, I may bring harmony—that where there is error, I may bring truth—that where there is doubt, I may bring faith—that where there is despair, I may bring hope—that where there are shadows, I may bring light—that where there is sadness, I may bring joy. Lord, grant that I may seek rather to comfort than to be comforted—to understand than to be understood—to love than to be loved. For it is by self-forgetting that one finds. It is by forgiving that one is forgiven. It is by dying that one awakens to Eternal Life. Amen."

Lord's Prayer: "Our Father, who art in heaven, hallowed be thy name. Thy kingdom come, Thy will be done, on earth as it is in heaven. Give us this day our daily bread and forgive us our trespasses as we forgive those who trespass against us. Lead us not into temptation, but deliver us from evil. For

Thine is the kingdom, and the power and the glory, forever. Amen."

Serenity Prayer: "God grant me the serenity the accept the things I cannot change, the courage to change the things I can, and the wisdom to know the difference."

Appendix C: 12-Step Program National Addresses

Alcoholics Anonymous World Services (AA)
475 Riverside Dr.
New York, NY 10163
(212) 870–3400
FAX (212) 870–3003

Al-Anon Family Group Headquarters, Inc.
P.O. Box 862, Midtown Station
New York, NY 10018–0862
(212) 302–7240
FAX (212) 869–3757
www.alanon.alateen.org

Adult Children Anonymous, Region 8 (ACA)
P.O. Box 150331
Arlington, TX 76015
(817) 478–3191

Cocaine Anonymous World Services (CAWS)
3740 Overland Ave., Suite H
P.O. Box 2000
Los Angeles, CA 90034–63377

(310) 559–5833
FAX (310) 559–2554

Co-Dependents Anonymous (CoDA)
P.O. Box 33577
Phoenix, AZ 85067–3577
(602) 277–7991
FAX (602) 274–6111

Debtors Anonymous (DA)
P.O. Box 400, Grand Central Station
New York, NY 10163–0400
(212) 642–8220

Food Addicts Anonymous (FAA)
108 Rutland
West Palm Beach, FL 34405
(407) 586–8985

Gamblers Anonymous (GA)
P.O. Box 17173
Los Angeles, CA 90017
(213) 386–8789

NarAnon World Service Office
P.O. Box 2562
Palos Verdes, CA 90274
(310) 547–5800

Narcotics Anonymous (NA)
Box 9999
Van Nuys, CA 91409
(818) 773–9999

Overeaters Anonymous (OA)
6070 Zenith Ct. NE
Rio Rancho, NM 87124–6424
(505) 891–2664

Sex Addicts Anonymous (SAA)
P.O. Box 70949

Houston, TX 77270
(713) 869–4902

Sex and Love Addicts Anonymous (SLAA)
The Augustine Fellowship
P.O. Box 650010
West Newton, MA 02165–0010
(617) 332–1845

Sexaholics Anonymous (SA)
P.O. Box 111910
Nashville, TN 37222
(615) 331–6230
FAX (615)331–6901

Sexual Compulsives Anonymous (SCA)
P.O. Box 1585
Old Chelsea Station
New York, NY 10013–0935
(800) 977–HEAL
(212) 606–3778 in NY

Appendix D: The 12 Steps

Step One: "We admitted we were powerless over alcohol [food; gambling; sex; relationships; tobacco; or people, places, and things, etc.]—that our lives had become unmanageable."

Step Two: "Came to believe that a Power greater than ourselves could restore us to sanity."

Step Three: "Made a decision to turn our will and our lives over to the care of God *as we understood Him.*"

Step Four: "Made a searching and fearless inventory of ourselves."

Step Five: "Admitted to God, to ourselves, and to another human being the exact nature of our wrongs."

Step Six: "Were entirely ready to have God remove all these defects of character."

Step Seven: "Humbly asked Him to remove our shortcomings."

Step Eight: "Made a list of all the persons we had harmed and became willing to make amends to them all."

Step Nine: "Made direct amends wherever possible, except when to do so would injure them or others."

Step Ten: "Continued to take personal inventory and when we were wrong promptly admitted it."

Step Eleven: "Sought through prayer and meditation to improve our conscious contact with God *as we understood Him*, praying only for knowledge of His will for us and the power to carry that out."

Step Twelve: "Having had a spiritual awakening as the result of these steps, we tried to carry this message to alcoholics [overeaters, gamblers, sex addicts, adult children of alcoholics, etc.] and to practice these principles in all our affairs."

Suggested Reading

GENERAL

Flores, P. J. (1997). *Group psychotherapy with addicted populations: An integration of twelve-step and psychodynamic theory.* New York: Haworth Press.

Miller, W. R. & Rollnick, S. (1991). *Motivational interviewing: Preparing people to change addictive behavior.* New York: Guilford Press.

Nakken, C. (1996). *The addictive personality.* Center City, MN: Hazelden Educational Materials.

Vannicelli, M. (1992). *Removing the roadblocks: Group psychotherapy with substance abusers and family members.* New York: Guilford Press.

CHEMICAL DEPENDENCY

Alcoholics Anonymous. (1939). *Alcoholics anonymous.* New York: Alcoholics Anonymous World Services.

Alcoholics Anonymous. (1953). *Twelve steps and twelve traditions.* New York: Alcoholics Anonymous World Services.

Bratter, T. & Forrest, G. (1985). *Alcoholism and substance abuse: Strategies for clinical intervention.* New York: The Free Press.

Brown, S. (1985). *Treating the alcoholic: A developmental model of recovery.* New York: John Wiley and Sons.

Finnegan, J. & Gray, D. (1990). *Recovery from addiction.* Berkeley, CA: Celestial Arts.

Goode, E. (1992). *Drugs in American Society.* New York: McGraw Hill.

Gorski, T. (1989). *Passages through recovery.* Center City, MN: Hazelden Educational Materials.

Hamilton, B. (1995). *Getting started in AA.* Center City, MN: Hazelden Educational Materials.

Mumey, J. (1994). *The new joy of being sober.* Minneapolis, MN: Deaconness Press.

Royce, J. E. (1989). *Alcohol problems and alcoholism: A comprehensive survey.* New York: The Free Press.

Twerski, A. (1997). *Addictive thinking.* Center City, MN: Hazelden Educational Materials.

EATING DISORDERS

Bill, B. (1981). *Compulsive overeater.* Center City, MN: Hazelden Educational Materials.

Chernin, K. (1994). *The hungry self: Women, eating, and identity.* New York: HarperPerennial.

Chernin, K. (1994). *The obsession.* New York: HarperPerennial.

Jackson, B. L. (1990). *Dieting: A dry drunk.* San Diego, CA: BJ Nautilus Publications.

Pipher, M. (1995). *Hunger pains.* New York: Ballantine Books.

Roth, G. (1993). *Breaking free from compulsive overeating.* New York: Plume Books.

Roth, G. (1993). *Feeding the hungry heart.* New York: Plume Books.

Roth, G. (1992). *When food is love.* New York: Plume Books.

Shepard, K. (1989). *Food addiction: The body knows.* Deerfield Beach, FL: Health Communications Inc.

Sours, J. A. (1992). *Starving to death in a sea of objects.* Northvale, NJ: Jason Aronson, Inc.

FAMILY/CO-DEPENDENCY

Bradshaw, J. (1995). *Family secrets: The path to self-acceptance.* New York: Bantam Books.

Bradshaw, J. (1993). *Healing the shame that binds you.* Deerfield Beach, FL: Health Communications.

Brown, S. (1998). *Treating adult children of alcoholics: A developmental perspective.* New York: John Wiley & Sons.

Cermack, T. (1986). *Diagnosing and treating co-dependence.* Minneapolis: Johnson Institute Books.

Friel, J. & Friel, L. (1988). *Adult children: The secrets of dysfunctional families.* Deerfield Beach, FL: Health Communications.

Melody, P. (1992). *Facing love addiction.* San Francisco: Harpers San Francisco.

Steinglass, P., Bennett, L., Wolin, S., & Russ, D. (1987). *The alcoholic family.* New York: Basic Books.

Wegschieder-Cruse, S. (1989). *Another chance: Hope and health for the alcoholic family.* Palto Alto, CA: Science and Behavioral Books.

Woititz, J. (1993). *Adult children of alcoholics.* Deerfield Beach, FL: Health Communications.

SEXUAL ADDICTION

Carnes, P. (1989). *Contrary to love: Helping the sexual addict.* Center City, MN: Hazelden Educational Materials.

Carnes, P. (1992). *Out of the shadows.* Center City, MN: Hazelden Educational Materials.

Carnes, P. (1992). *Sexual anorexia.* Center City, MN: Hazelden Educational Materials.

Sexaholics Anonymous. (1989). *Sexaholics anonymous.* SA Literature.

Sex and Love Addicts Anonymous. (1986). *Sex and love addicts anonymous.* Boston: The Augustine Fellowship.

Index

About the Authors

JAN PARKER is Assistant Professor and Lead Program Faculty in the Department of Psychology at National University in San Diego, where she has taught for 15 years. She is a licensed psychotherapist in private practice in Poway, CA and has worked with clients affected by addictive disorders for 20 years.

DIANA L. GUEST is a licensed psychotherapist in private practice in San Diego, and is the clinical director of a nonprofit social agency, as well as an adjunct professor at National University.